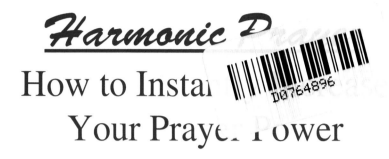

How to Insta~~ll~~
Your Praye~~r~~ Power

Alan Tutt

Author of:

Choose To Believe: A Practical Guide to Living Your Dreams
Prosperity From the Inside Out
Treasure Map to Online Riches

Creator of:

EmBRACES Belief Entrainment System

PowerKeys Publishing
1805 Walker Ave NW
Grand Rapids, MI 49504
www.PowerKeysPub.com

Harmonic Prayer
How to Instantly Increase Your Prayer Power
www.HarmonicPrayer.com

Produced using OpenOffice Software from OpenOffice.org
Cover design by Alan Tutt produced using CorelDraw.
Cover Photo by Alan Tutt.

Printed in the USA

PowerKeys Publishing
1805 Walker Ave NW
Grand Rapids, MI 49504
www.PowerKeysPub.com
sales@powerkeyspub.com

Special Quantity Discounts

PowerKeys Publishing offers special quantity discounts, making our books ideal for sales premiums, corporate gifts, fund raising, and more. Special customized versions are also available for specific needs. Contact our Special Sales Department at the addresses above for details.

LEGAL DISCLAIMER

Neither the publisher nor the author are engaged in dispensing medical advice or prescribing the use of any technique as a form of treatment for physical, emotional, or medical problems without the advice of a physician, either directly or indirectly. In the event you use any of the information in this book for yourself, which is your constitutional right, the author and publisher assume no responsibility for your actions. If you do not agree to be bound by these terms, please return the book for a refund.

Harmonic Prayer

How to Instantly Increase Your Prayer Power

Alan Tutt

Table of Contents

Chapter 1:
Setting the Foundation

E verybody prays. Not everyone gets the results they should. This book explains why you may not be getting the results you should from your prayers, and what you can do to get miraculous results every time you pray.

What's missing in your life? Love, health, wealth, protection, peace, respect, a feeling of being useful to the world? Whatever you want and need in your life can be yours when you learn how to use Harmonic Prayer—with faith, focus, and a feeling of harmony with God.

Not only will you see better results instantly, but with continued practice, you'll reach new levels of joy and satisfaction as you grow spiritually.

Throughout history, mystics and spiritual leaders have told us that God answers prayers, and that the key factor is our faith.

> *"According to your faith is it done to you."*
> *— Matthew 9:29*

> *"And he did not do many miracles there because of their lack of faith."*
> *— Matthew 13:58*

> *"I tell you the truth, if anyone says to this mountain, 'Go, throw yourself into the sea,' and does not doubt in his heart but believes that what he says will happen, it will be done for him."*
> *— Mark 11:23*

> *"Everything is possible for him who believes."*
> *— Mark 9:23*

> *"I tell you the truth, anyone who has faith in me will do what I have been doing. He will do even greater things than these, because I am going to the Father." — John 14:12*

In the quotes above from the Christian Bible, we are told that not only is our faith responsible for the results we get from prayer, but that Christ Himself could not perform miracles where there was a lack of faith.

These quotes also indicate that there are literally no limits to what we may do with prayer. Not only can we do everything that Christ Himself did, but even more as well!

> *Although I have included a number of quotes from the Christian Bible, you do not need to be a Christian to get positive results from prayer. Harmonic Prayer works just as well if you follow other religions, or no particular religion at all.*

Some modern spiritual leaders have suggested that only certain things may be asked for in prayer. They suggest that it's wrong to ask for money, for example. As the quotes above indicate, this is not true. You may ask for anything.

However, as we will cover in more detail later, you may get more satisfactory results asking for some things rather than others. As a quick example—rather than asking for one specific person to fall in love with you, you may be much happier asking for "true love." The person you select on your own may not be the best partner for you, and may actually make your life a living hell!

Because faith is such an important factor in prayer, some prayers tend to produce the exact opposite of what you want. This usually happens when you are not fully aware of the inner motivations behind a desire. As you will learn later in this book, WHY you pray for something is much more important that WHAT you pray for.

As an example, praying for a million dollars may seem to be a good way to produce abundant wealth and a comfortable life. However, the desire to stockpile large amounts of money usually comes from a fear mentality (greed), indicating a lack of faith in what many New Thought people call "everlasting supply."

For this reason, it's usually smarter to pray for the essence of what you want, because God knows a lot more than any of us. In Chapter 8, we'll cover the types of requests that tend to produce the results you really want in your life.

What Makes Me an Expert on Prayer?

Although I am not ordained into any organized religion, I have lived my whole life with prayer, and have dedicated myself to learning the true nature of prayer and what makes it work.

It all began at an early age. I remember going to Sunday school as a boy and hearing stories about how Christ and the prophets performed miracles, such as changing water into wine, parting the Red Sea, healing the sick, and even raising the dead. Those stories stuck with me, and continued to pique my interest.

Sometime during my high school years, I prayed that God would teach me the truth behind miracles, promising to teach others what I learned. At that time of my life, everything looked great. I was a straight-A student, had earned a full-tuition scholarship to DeVry University for Electrical Engineering, and was headed for a career in a highly profitable field in which I had great interest and enthusiasm.

For a variety of reasons, I found myself failing at DeVry. I was trying to work full time while going to school full time, and couldn't manage my time effectively. I started sleeping late, missing classes, and my scholastic career was quickly coming to an end.

Eventually, I dropped out.

For someone who had always done well in school, this was a monumental failure. The rest of my life came crashing down like a house of cards. Eventually, I hit bottom. No home, no car, no money, no job, no friends, and no one I could ask for help. As I left town (on foot), I found a penny on the ground, which was the ONLY money I had at that time.

I was truly starting over with nothing.

The Discovery That Changed Everything

In high school, my interest in miracles led me to delve into ESP and similar topics. As my life tumbled downhill, I started grasping at anything that promised to teach me how to tap into the power of miracles.

I read the Bible, and other than a series of generic suggestions to "have faith," there wasn't anything there which explained HOW to do that.

I turned to books on other religions, ESP, astrology, mysticism, magick, and even witchcraft, looking for some clue that would help me turn my life around and get it back on course with the vision of success I felt I deserved. In the course of a single year, I had read (at least a part of) several hundred books.

Nothing seemed to help, until one morning, after wandering the streets all night, I walked into a bookstore to get out of the cold, and found *The Miracle of Mind Dynamics* by Joseph Murphy, who instantly became my favorite author!

As I stood there reading the words on the page, I felt an incredible sensation rise up within me. I learned to pretend that my prayer was already answered, and to *feel its reality within the moment.* (This was a suggestion I never found in the Bible.) Instantly, I felt my whole body relax, and bursting forth was this unbelievable feeling of joy and satisfaction as I imagined that I would be given enough money to rent a place and get back on my feet again.

That was about 10:30 in the morning. About 4:30 that afternoon, I received the results of my prayer when I found $70 on the sidewalk! With this sudden windfall, I was able to rent a cheap room for a week (*very* cheap, and *very* run down) and get a little food to keep going.

The very next day, I went back to the bookstore and bought three of Joseph Murphy's books, *The Miracle of Mind Dynamics* (the one I read in the store), *The Power of Your Subconscious Mind*, and *Your Infinite Power to be Rich*.

Today I own 14 of his books, with multiple copies of some of them. I like to buy multiple copies so I can give them away when I feel someone needs what the book offers.

Experiments in Prayer

Most of the time, I would experiment with simple things that didn't involve other people, like changing the weather. There was one summer in particular when I was living with someone who had a small garden and didn't want to water it every day. At one point, she commented that it would be nice if it rained a little each day. A few minutes of thoughtful action did the trick. Every day for the next three months, a small amount of rain would fall from the skies.

During the same time period, a tornado was reported to be heading in our direction. When I saw my girlfriend running around to collect her animals, I told her to calm down and that I would pray about it. I sat down, focused my mind on dispersing the tornado, and within a matter of minutes, the news station reported that the tornado had dissipated.

Because I lacked faith in prosperity back then, my prayers for money rarely worked. There were a few successes, though. One such success occurred when I worked at a die-cutting shop, a place that does finishing work for printers. As a day-laborer hired merely to do odd jobs, I had absolutely no control over the amount of work that came into the shop, yet I was able to consistently get the specific number of hours I wanted each week. Each week, I picked a different number, such as 40, 45, 42, 46.5, or 49. At the end of each week, my timesheet was consistently within a half-hour of what I specified to myself at the beginning of that week.

I'll never forget the time I was talking to one of the press operators about this and mentioned how I had decided I would get 48 hours that week. His reaction was, "We don't even have enough work to keep us busy for 40 hours. There's no way we'll get 8 hours of overtime!" I smiled and simply said, "We have no idea what other jobs are coming into the shop. We can only see what's here now. There will be more jobs coming in the next few days."

The other press operator (we had only two presses operating on second shift) thought the idea was intriguing and was open to the possibility. Within a couple of days, a large job came into the shop, which required foil stamping and needed to be out the same week. End result: the first press operator only got 40 hours that week, yet the second operator and I got 48 hours, proving once again that my prayer process worked.

The next week, the second press operator and I were talking about this and he suggested we go for maximum overtime. I thought it would be an interesting experiment and prayed by setting my intention accordingly. (Without a doubt, the SIMPLEST form of prayer possible.) By this time, my faith was so strong, I KNEW something special was going to happen.

Maximum overtime turned out to be 60 to 70 hour weeks for months on end! That special rush job was done so well we ended up getting far more work from it than we bargained for! My paychecks were FAT to say the least! I was smiling regularly for the first time in years.

Notice here that I was not running a business. Nor was I a salesperson in this company. I was simply a day-laborer brought in to fill a low-level position. I also wasn't asking God to make things happen for me. I simply "decided" what I wanted, and felt assured—had faith—that I would get it. I didn't spend any time during the week thinking about whether I would get what I wanted or not, nor did I question the process. Once I set it in motion, I let it go and only checked at the end to verify that my timesheet matched what I had specified.

From the many experiments I performed, I had solid proof that I could get the results I wanted from prayer. Exactly how this worked was still a matter of debate, and I continued to test many different techniques and combinations of techniques for years afterwards.

Despite many suggestions that faith was the only requirement for prayer, my experiments led me to conclude that there were three keys to unlock the power of miracles. I knew that faith was one of those factors, but I also found that mental focus was a factor, as well as something I now call "harmonic resonance with God."

All of these factors will be discussed in depth in this book.

Relationship Success

One of the most enjoyable results of prayer is the wonderful relationship I have with my wife, Linda. When I decided it was time to pray for the "perfect" relationship, I started by looking at the beliefs I had about relationships, and considered how I could increase my faith in this area.

I would say that the most important new beliefs were: 1) as long as I use prayer to create what I want, my life will always get better, and 2) every relationship is like a walk in the woods—sometimes you run into brier patches, but if you continue, you get to see glorious splendors. Both beliefs are based on faith—faith that there will be good times ahead.

Once I knew what new beliefs would support my prayers, I began working with self-hypnosis. *(I would use a different process now.)* I spent a few sessions a week programming the new beliefs into my mind so my reaction patterns would support the goal I set. Then, I started performing a form of prayer I call creative daydreaming.

In those sessions, I would enter a light to medium level meditative state. While in that state, I would affirm "I am now creating the future I want, and the images I play in my mind will manifest into my life. My inner mind knows the best way for this to happen, and it brings this about in the best way possible." *(Again, I would do it differently today.)*

For the next period of time (probably about 10 – 20 minutes), I would daydream about the relationship I wanted. I saw myself meeting someone who attracted me, and I saw her being attracted to me as well. I saw us spending lots of time together, and while seeing these things, I felt the emotions I knew I would feel when the events actually happened. I felt the most intense feeling of love I could imagine feeling. I felt the emotion of happiness, the emotion of desire, and all the other emotions that fill a good relationship. And yes, I daydreamed about wonderful sex.

After each session, I would feel very much at peace. There may have been a slight feeling of emptiness since the relationship was not there at the time, but I felt as if it would come soon enough. In essence, I felt as if I had spent some quality time with the woman of my dreams, and although she was gone, she would return later.

I continued to work with these prayer sessions nearly every day for several weeks. Then I had to focus on other tasks, so I let it go. (This was during a period of rebuilding my life after some failed experiments.) In a few months, I met Linda, who is now my wife. As soon as I met her, I knew she was the one. Virtually everything I visualized, including many elements I had never experienced in a relationship, are now a part of our life together.

Business Success

As you may recall, my life took a major downturn after I left high school, to the point where I became homeless. Living in such desperate circumstances proved to be a major handicap, as I quickly lost any faith in my ability to succeed. (Probably why we have the saying, "The rich get richer, and the poor get poorer.")

Although I had experienced limited success in financial matters, such as in the die-cutting shop example, true prosperity continued to elude me for many years. *(If I had only known then what I know now....)*

Over time, I discovered several techniques to build my faith (discussed later in this book), and the more I used them, the more my results improved.

Along the way, I also learned photography. Eventually, I started working for Lifetouch doing school pictures, Olan Mills doing portraits, and a local company doing weddings. I also started pursuing freelance work in my free time.

All while praying that I would be successful.

A breakthrough came after I created my own "not-so-subliminal" tape to help reprogram my inner beliefs about money and success in general. I simply recorded myself repeating dozens of positive statements about what I thought were important beliefs to have. When I played the tape in the background while doing other things, it became subliminal since I wasn't focused on listening to the recording.

Within a few months, I was making good money as a photographer, and having a great time doing it. In fact, there were some jobs where I walked away with the equivalent of $1,000 for each hour I was there!

An even bigger breakthrough came when I prayed again for increased prosperity. In those prayers, I imagined owning a business which paid me a large, regular income and didn't require my personal involvement on a day-to-day basis. As I exercised, I pretended that my company was being handled by employees, and when the phone rang, I pretended it was a big order coming in.

At the time, I had no idea what kind of business it would be, but I knew it could happen simply because I was praying for it.

In the following months, I started noticing many suggestions to start a business on the Internet. I had no idea how to create a website, and frankly, I didn't want to learn, so I resisted the idea. However, the more the idea was suggested to me, the more I realized that God was trying to tell me something.

What got me off my butt and online was an idea I heard while listening to the audio version of *One Minute Millionaire* by Robert G. Allen and Mark Victor Hansen. I heard that there were website services to help you create an instant Internet storefront using a point-and-click interface.

The idea intrigued me, especially since the authors claimed it would generate a passive income with no day-to-day personal involvement. Although the resources they listed were no longer available, and the process wasn't as easy as they said, I did find a way to set up a website using a point-and-click interface. And thus, my first website (www.KeysToPower.com) was born. *(It's changed a lot since then.)*

One thing led to the next, and within a month, I was making money online. The more I learned, the more money I made. The nature of the Internet allows quick, cheap testing of advertising, impossible in any other form of business. And although I made many mistakes and spent a ton of money on my education (buying ebooks, software, and marketing courses), the business was "in the black" (had earned more than I had spent) in less than 6 months. Almost impossible with any off-line business!

Over the years, my prayers have continued to produce tangible results. My relationship with Linda keeps getting better and better. My business grows more profitable, and has brought in as much as $5,000 in a single day.

Now, I get to spend my days the way I want, and life is good.

What Is Prayer?

Some people think of prayer as a process of kneeling down beside their bed at night to talk to God. Others think of prayer as a sacred ritual using candles, incense, and a mantra chanted over and over again for long periods of time. Still others think of prayer as a scientific process of tapping into and directing Universal Powers using specially charged implements, such as talismans and amulets, in a process some call magick.

For the purpose of this book, I'm going to define prayer as a process of asking for Divine Assistance to fulfill specified desires. This is a very open definition which encompasses many different methods of prayer.

Any method of prayer may be used as long as it fulfills certain requirements, which we'll cover in detail in the next chapter.

What (or Who) Is God?

Many people see God as some type of "super human," with desires, plans, and personality, and while this may be okay, I think it limits God in countless ways.

Many others have found God to respond so predictably that we could consider God to be a natural force of the Universe, much like gravity, electricity, or nuclear energy. Again, while this may be okay, I think it also limits God in many ways.

And depending on what cultures you've experienced, you may be familiar with different names often used for God, such as Yahweh, Allah, Elohim, Adi Purush, Bhagwaan, Brahma, Ishvar, Maheshvar, Vishnu, Krishna, Rama, Waheguru, Ek Onkar, Satnam, Nirankar, Akal Purakh, or any of countless others.

Personally, I think it's impossible for any human to really define God, simply because we cannot possibly understand everything that God is. However, for the purpose of this book, I'm going to define God as the Divine Essence of the Universe, the Eternal Source from which all things flow.

In the end, God is what God is. ("I AM THAT I AM") As human beings, we do not have the capacity to fully understand God, and so it's best to allow God to reveal God's nature to us as God chooses. *(I apologize for the awkward language. God is neither strictly male nor strictly female, neither a 'he' nor a 'she', and the English language does not yet have a dual-gender pronoun, meaning "both male and female.")*

Why Does God Answer Prayers?

In order to get positive results from prayer, it's important to enter prayer with a solid expectation that your prayer will be answered.. So let's take a moment and discuss the possible reasons why God would answer prayer.

If you choose to see God as a "super human" type of being, then you might see the prayer process as one where God hears your request, delegates the task of manifesting it to an angel or other heavenly being, who in turn goes to work to fulfill your desires.

From this viewpoint, you could say that God acts as a loving parent, doing whatever is required to help you live a happy and successful life, just as any *loving* parent would do. At times, this may mean that God will deny a request, because fulfilling it would somehow hurt you. It also means that when you ask for love, you will get love, even if it comes from a different source than you originally expected.

If you approach life with a more scientific view—choosing to see God as a natural force of the Universe—you might prefer to see prayer as a process where a vibration is established in a universal field, which produces the final manifestation in a more-or-less mechanical fashion. This is the typical explanation for New Age ideas, such as the Law of Attraction.

With this view of God, the reason for God answering a prayer becomes similar to the reason for hydrogen and oxygen to combine and form water—it just happens. This means that in order to get the results you want from prayer, you must pay attention to the variables in a "prayer formula" and make sure that all requirements are met, such as faith, focus, and a feeling of harmony with God, as described in this book.

Because we, as humans, cannot know the true nature of God, we also cannot know exactly how prayer works. Luckily, both of the viewpoints described above will produce positive results from prayer, because, for whatever reason, God DOES answer prayers when those prayers are offered with faith, focus, and a feeling of Divine Harmony.

What Is Successful Prayer?

If we are to approach prayer in a practical way, we must have a practical way to measure success. In the case of prayer, where our intention is to produce a specific result, determining success is easy. Did we get the result we asked for?

Of course, we may want to consider other factors as well. How quickly must the prayer be answered, for instance, before we attribute the result to our prayer? Must the manifestation of our objective break the laws of physics before it can be considered a direct result of prayer? Does an angel have to appear before you?

Personally, I take a very pragmatic view. If you pray for something and get it within a reasonable time, your prayer was answered. For example, if you pray for a new car, and later discover that you can afford the payments with your current income, your prayer was answered. The fact that you already had the available funds simply means your prayer was answered before you even prayed about it.

On the other hand, if you've been praying for romantic adventures, and nothing has happened for several months, it's time to consider if your prayer process is working as it should.

What Can You Expect?

Most of the time, prayers are answered through what may be considered a normal course of events. Rarely will there be any bolts of lightning, or choirs of angels singing.

Let's say you pray for a new relationship. The next day, you get frustrated at a co-worker, and go for a drive. An hour later, you stop to get something to drink. Before you get back into your car, you notice a ball game, and decide to sit and watch. While there, you "just happen" to meet someone, and as you talk, you find yourself wanting to get to know this person better. One thing leads to another, and a new relationship is formed. Whether you realized it or not, God guided you every step of the way so you could meet this person.

Divine Guidance can usually be described as a string of events and intuitive feelings leading you to do things you wouldn't ordinarily do. When God guides you, God will do whatever is necessary to get you there.

If you are open to intuition (which is just as common in men as it is in women), God will use this channel to communicate with you. However, if you block your intuition—either consciously or unconsciously—then God will create physical events which will "push your buttons" or give you "a kick in the backside" to get you moving in the right direction.

You may also receive Divine Guidance through your dreams. Here, it's important to realize that any "symbolism" used in your dreams will be relatively easy for you to interpret, because the message was intended specifically for you. If you wake up with any strong dream after praying, spend a little time to figure out what it may mean to you, and how it may apply to your prayers.

Any time you pay attention to your dreams, you'll start to remember more of them. This can be an excellent way to get in touch with your deeper self, as you become more familiar with the imagery and themes that appear in your dreams. You may find it helpful to keep a notepad near your bed so you can jot down notes to help you remember your dreams later. It's amazing how quickly a vivid dream will fade into oblivion if it's not written down.

If you cannot find any meaning in a dream, don't worry about it. Not every dream has meaning, and some dreams are simply our inner minds working things out. When God sends you a message, God will make it SO CLEAR that you cannot possibly miss it.

Divine Guidance isn't the only way that prayers are answered. Sometimes God changes the way other people behave.

If you pray to find harmony in a relationship with a co-worker, for example, you may go into work to find your co-worker in an unusually pleasant mood. And this may be the spark that nudges things into a more positive direction, eventually blossoming into a wonderfully harmonious working relationship.

There really are no set rules about how God answers prayers, and anything—literally, *anything*—can happen. And yes, that includes true miracles coming out of nowhere to answer your prayers. You just need to know how to do Harmonic Prayer.

How to Get Maximum Results Quickly

This book is organized to help you get results as quickly as possible—even BEFORE you're done reading it.

In the next chapter, you'll learn about the Harmonic Prayer process, which will improve your results right away. Just by following the Harmonic Prayer process, you can double or triple your prayer power. In Chapter 3, you'll learn more ways you can *instantly* increase the power of your prayers.

Each successive chapter gives you additional techniques which further increase the power of your prayers, but which also take more time. For example, Chapter 4 talks about meditation, which requires at least 20 minutes, and Chapters 5 & 6 talk about a process for discovering and changing limiting beliefs, which can sometimes take an hour or more.

Only after all of the "quick fixes" have been covered do we get into longer-term strategies to increase your prayer power to the Nth degree.

As you go through this book, practice the various techniques described. Reading about them will do nothing for you. It's only when you work with them that they will increase your prayer power.

Chapter 2:
The Harmonic Prayer Process

In this chapter, I'll describe the essence of the Harmonic Prayer process. This process is based on the primary factors I've found to be responsible for effective prayer, which are faith, focus, and a feeling of harmony with God.

In the following chapters, we'll discuss how you can improve each of these factors to make your prayers even more powerful.

The steps outlined below do not need to be complicated, and each step may be completed in just a few seconds. If you want to spend more time on one or more of these steps, that's okay too.

For quick reference, the steps involved are:

1. Harmonize with God
2. Activate your faith
3. Focus on what you want
4. Give thanks
5. Follow Divine Guidance

Step 1: Harmonize With God

This is the starting point for effective prayer. Unless you are in harmony with God, your prayer will go nowhere, and nothing will happen. To be in harmony with God is one of the best feelings you can ever experience. It's better than drugs or sex, and can be a very healthy addiction.

One of the quickest and easiest ways to bring yourself into harmony with God is to love. Love life, love yourself, love everyone, love nature, love the Universe, and above all, love God.

This is one of the main reasons Christ taught love as a way of life. The more you love, the more you are in harmony with God, and the more powerful your prayers will be. The more you engage in hate, envy, greed, and pride, the weaker your prayers become.

If anything is happening in your life that makes it difficult to feel love, the best advice I can give you is to ignore it (as best you can) for the few minutes it takes to pray for a solution.

Focus on anything and everything you CAN feel love for, and spend as much time as necessary (or as much time as you have available) to bring yourself into harmony with God. A little is good, a lot is better. In Chapter 4, I'll give you a few short meditations that will help with this.

Personally, when I pray, the first thing I do is to imagine God as a HUGE entity standing in front of me, and I imagine myself giving God a great big hug. As I do this, I also make a conscious effort to open myself spiritually to accept God into my being.

This results in an incredible rush of joy and satisfaction that makes every part of my body tingle, both inside and out. That's when I know that I am in harmony with God.

The more you practice opening yourself up to God and allowing God to fill your being, the easier it will be, and the better results you'll get.

Step 2: Activate Your Faith

Faith is the power which makes prayer work. As Christ often said, "according to your faith is it done to you." The stronger your faith, the better your prayers will work. With absolute faith (faith without any doubt whatsoever—a "knowingness"), true miracles are possible.

In the next several chapters, we'll go into much more detail on how to increase your faith during prayer. For now, realize that the easiest way to activate your faith is to think of something you know to be an absolute fact, such as the reality of your own hand, or the fact that you need God's help.

By thinking about something you KNOW to be true, a feeling of trust, confidence, and faith wells up within you, and you can bring this feeling into the rest of your prayer process. Once you feel faith welling up, you can also imagine "turning up the volume" on your faith, and by doing so, you can increase your faith even more. Again, we'll go into more detail on this in the following chapters.

Ideally, you want to have absolute faith in the Harmonic Prayer process itself, and in the results that God will ultimately create for you. You'll know when you've reached this point because you'll experience something I call "Divine Detachment"—a feeling that the problem is already solved, and the solution will manifest no matter what you do.

When you're first starting out, this may not be easy, since you have no real experience with getting results from prayer. However, by eliciting a feeling of faith about other things, you can essentially "borrow" this faith and "transfer" it to the Harmonic Prayer process.

As you begin to notice better and better results from your prayers, you will naturally gain faith in the Harmonic Prayer process itself, and before long, you'll KNOW that your prayers will produce results—even miraculous results if necessary.

Step 3: Focus on What You Want

This is the step where you make your request known to God. You can do this with words, with mental images, or with actions. The form is not as important as the intention behind it.

It's important that you communicate your intention clearly. To do this well, you need to focus your mind on what you want, and avoid all other thoughts during the Harmonic Prayer process.

You don't need to include every detail about how your prayer should manifest. You want to leave it open for God to give you the best possible result, unhampered by limited human thinking.

Rather, you want to be very clear about what you want to happen. If you want a mountain to throw itself into the sea, you want to be clear about WHICH mountain is thrown into WHICH sea, and that no-one gets hurt in the process.

If you want a new romantic relationship, you want to be clear about what type of person you want, the types of activities the two of you will enjoy doing together, and any other details you want to be part of the new relationship.

If you're looking for a new job, you want to be very clear about the type of job you want. If the only thing you really care about is that you enjoy the work, whatever it is, then you want to be clear about the FEELINGS the new job will give you.

When you pray, you'll find the process will work better if you can imagine your request as you speak the words describing it. This combination of imagination and spoken words seems to help focus your mind to an incredible degree, and will make your prayers even more powerful.

Step 4: Give Thanks

Giving thanks is a great way to end the Harmonic Prayer process. Not only does it ease your transition to other things, it also brings you into greater harmony with God. And ending your Harmonic Prayer this way makes it even more powerful.

There are many folks who feel that spending time in gratitude is the best thing you can do to improve your life. The logic here is that the more you are in harmony with God, the more God will guide the events of your life to a state of perfection and grace.

The same can be said about love. The more you love, the more you are in harmony with God, and the more your life will reflect love back to you.

Love and gratitude are two very powerful forces. Forces that produce astounding and miraculous results.

Step 5: Follow Divine Guidance

After you've prayed, your task is to follow Divine Guidance. In most cases, your prayer will be answered with a set of instructions—given one at a time—that will lead you to the outcome you asked for.

And while God is certainly more than capable of guiding you without your help, you'll find it a lot easier—and more enjoyable—if you actively participate in the process.

A great way to listen for God's guidance is with meditation. After you've finished praying, stay right where you are, and quiet your mind. Don't strain for the answer. Just keep your mind open, and pay attention to the thoughts that come into your mind.

Not all of the thoughts which come into your mind will be from God. Some may be from your own subconscious mind, especially when you're new to the process.

The best thing I can tell you is that there will be a slight difference between thoughts which come from God and thoughts which do not. It's not that you'll hear angels singing, thunder cracking, or see a shaft of light beaming down from the skies. The difference will usually be small, like a feeling in your gut, or a tiny vibration which resonates at a different frequency.

With practice and experience, you'll learn to distinguish which thoughts are worth paying attention to, and which ones should be ignored. The more you trust the process (ie.— have faith), the sooner you'll notice the difference.

If you don't get anything definite right away, don't worry. Trust that God will answer your prayer in Divine Order—meaning that it will happen at the soonest possible opportunity, when the conditions are right.

As you go about your life, you may notice events that "push" or "pull" you in one way or another. This is another form of Divine Guidance, and being open to new directions will help God answer your prayers.

Getting Direct Answers from God

Another way to get Divine Guidance is to "cast lots" for the answer. This process was used in Biblical times when important decisions had to be made. *(See Acts 1:24 – 26 for an example.)*

Essentially, you pray for an answer to a question, then set up a "random" event to indicate God's answer. This could be flipping a coin, drawing straws, throwing dice, drawing cards, opening a book with eyes closed and placing a finger on a page, or anything else that can indicate Divine Guidance.

Keep in mind that the purpose is to receive an answer from God, so you want to be as much in harmony with God as you can during the process. Otherwise, you're just gambling.

The Bible has often been used for this. Here, you pray for the answer you need, then close your eyes, open the Bible to a "random" page, place a finger on a page, and finally look to see what is written under your finger. What you find there will indicate an answer to your question.

Other books can also be used. For example, if you have a problem in relationships, using a book on relationships can make it easier for God to give you a direct answer. You could also use the same process to select an appropriate book from several possible choices.

How Often Should You Pray?

Feel free to use the Harmonic Prayer process for anything and everything. Nothing is too small or too large to ask for God's help. And the more you pray, the better you get at it.

As a general rule, it's okay to pray whenever you feel the need, even if that means praying several times every hour.

Just realize that your prayers will be answered in God's time. If you find yourself wondering if the process is working, you may want to pray for greater faith.

Chapter 3: How to *Instantly* Increase Your Prayer Power

F aith, focus, and a feeling of harmony with God are the three primary keys to effective prayer. Increasing the strength of these keys leads to greater prayer power.

Although Christ taught that faith was the most important key to effective prayer, it has taken nearly 2000 years for the human race to learn how to deliberately develop faith, and more importantly, how to do so quickly.

As it stands, there are still many people today who teach that the only way to develop faith is to spend lots of time reading about Christ and His miracles. This process, discussed in Chapter 5, does eventually produce tangible results, however, it only works if you trust that the Christian Bible is a history of fact, and not allegorical fiction.

In this chapter, you will learn a variety of techniques that *instantly* increase your prayer power no matter what you currently believe. While they may at times seem obvious, history clearly shows that they were not.

In fact, the main reason I wrote this book was because I could not find ANYONE else teaching this material in the context of prayer.

Spiritual NLP

Many of the suggestions in this chapter are based on a science called NLP, or Neuro-Linguistic Programming. NLP was originally developed by Richard Bandler and John Grinder in the early 1970s. At its core, NLP is about finding out how successful people think, and modeling them to duplicate their success.

To do this, NLP students use a variety of mental tools, such as resource anchors, maps, filters, frames, representational systems, submodalities, strategies, pacing and leading, elicitation, and future pacing.

For the most part, NLP is taught as a system for personal development, habit control, and achieving success in business. Advertisers and salespeople all over the world use NLP techniques to persuade customers to buy more of their products. If you're interested in learning more about using NLP for persuasion, you may want to take a look at a course I wrote called *Keys To Power Persuasion*, available at www.PowerKeysPub.com/keys-to-power-persuasion.

When applied in the context of prayer, we will use several of the same techniques that are taught in the context of persuasion. Specifically, how to elicit the resource states of focus and trust (faith), and the use of something called "submodalities" to communicate clearly.

As you'll see for yourself, the tools of NLP may sound complicated, but are actually very simple things we use all the time. The magic of NLP is that it gives us conscious control over things we usually do without thinking.

Resource Anchors for Faith and Focus

Most of us feel more confident when we straighten our backs and display good posture, whether sitting or standing. Since confidence and faith are essentially the same thing, this is a quick and easy way to increase your faith during prayer.

The same can be said for breathing deeply. Taking a deep breath helps you feel more secure within yourself, which leads to an increase in both faith and focus.

Public speakers are taught that when they are nervous, a quick and easy way to focus their mind and feel more confident is to speak with a loud and firm voice.

The reason why these things increase our faith is because our minds have learned, over time and with repeated experience, to associate the actions with the feelings. When we feel confident, we typically stand taller, breathe deeper, and speak louder. When we feel fear, we tend to hunch over, breathe more shallowly, and speak with a softer voice. This pattern creates a mental association.

We can use this association in reverse, and elicit the desired mental states at will. Students of NLP call this "resource anchoring." An anchor in this context is nothing more than a mental association between a physical act and a feeling or thought.

For many people, bringing their hands together helps them focus, and may be why we are taught to do this when we pray. This action also tends to carry spiritual meaning, and increases the feeling of faith as well as focus.

This also happens with the act of kneeling, or standing in what is often called a "star position", where your feet are about shoulder-width apart, and your hands are hanging loose or stretched out to either side.

The specific position isn't important, although those who teach the star position will often say that you must face east, with palms facing forward, and they may possibly include other details as well. What is really important is that the physical act triggers a feeling of faith or focus. You could even pray while hopping on one foot and singing "Mary Had a Little Lamb," if that helps you focus.

The best anchors are things you do naturally. What do you tend to do when you feel confident? How do you carry yourself? Do you stand or sit? Do you relax, smile, chuckle, or move around more than when you feel afraid? Do you do anything special with your hands? Would you feel more confident that your prayers will be answered if a group prayed with you? How would being out in nature affect your faith and/or focus? If any of these help you focus or feel more confident, they can help you increase your prayer power.

Other resource anchors can be used to help you feel more spiritual, which as you can easily guess, is also good when praying. Such anchors may be as simple as holding a Bible or rosary, sitting in church or at a home altar with inspirational paintings, photos, and/or sculptures around you, lighting candles and incense, or even playing uplifting music. Resource anchors may be simple or more complex, with many things working together, as in a ceremony or ritual.

Whatever helps you feel more confident, more focused, and more spiritual can be used to get better results from prayer.

How I Use Resource Anchors

When I want to elicit a feeling of faith and focus, I turn my mind to things that are obviously real and true, such as the reality of the ground under my feet, or a physical object in front of me. With my focus "anchored" on the physical reality around me, I take a deep breath and let my mind clear as I exhale. As I do this, I also straighten my back, and let my body relax as well.

Within a matter of moments, I feel more solid, more grounded, more focused. I also feel a greater degree of faith—an excellent condition in which to pray.

To carry this further, I focus my mind on specific mental anchors—thoughts of things I consider absolute truths, and which may or may not be apparent in the space around me. Mental anchors work just like physical ones. When you trigger the anchored thought, a feeling of trust, confidence, and faith is also triggered as well.

Mental anchors may be very simple, like the thought that 2+2=4, or that the sky is blue. They can also be more complex, and include thoughts such as "God is good," "With God, all things are possible," or "Now is the only moment that matters."

Again, anything that helps you feel more focused, more confident, and more spiritual will make your prayers more powerful.

Associative Linking

The power of resource anchoring comes from the natural tendency our minds have to associate different things together, such as good posture with confidence.

Those who study an aspect of NLP called "conversational hypnosis" know that you can also inject a feeling of trust (another word for faith) in whatever you say simply by verbally linking a trustworthy statement with an idea you want the listener to accept.

This works in much the same way as resource anchors, with a somewhat different implementation.

In prayer, you can increase your own faith simply by referring to things you KNOW to be true.   Here are a few examples:

1. I ask this in the name of Christ, who said that anything we ask in his name will be done for us.
2. Because God is much bigger and more powerful than the entire Universe, this problem is solved in Divine Order.
3. Just as surely as the sun will rise tomorrow, I trust that God will do this for me.
4. Nature is full of great abundance. This abundance flows into my life now.

As with resource anchoring, the key here is that whatever you include in your prayer should trigger a feeling of faith, focus, and/or a feeling of harmony with God.

Submodality Modification

Something else you can do to instantly increase your prayer power is to pay attention to HOW you focus on the things you pray for. Once again, we're going to use a concept from NLP. In this case, the concept is known as "submodalities."

Although it may sound complicated, and you may need some practice before you master it, paying attention to submodalities during prayer soon becomes second nature.

Experts say that each of us has a preferred "modality" of thinking. Most of us are visual thinkers, and have a tendency to "see" thoughts, ideas, and feelings. Others are auditory and think in terms of sounds. A smaller number of folks are called kinesthetics because they relate to the world around them in terms of physical sensation. A very tiny minority focus on other modalities, known as gustatory and olfactory, and relate to the world by taste and smell respectively.

When you imagine the outcome you're praying for, you will tend to focus on one of these modalities more than the others. Each modality may be described with a number of details which NLP students call submodalities.

Take a moment and think about something you did recently. It could be talking to a friend, eating breakfast, or getting dressed in the morning. What do you notice first? Is it an image, a sound, a physical feeling, a smell, a taste, or is it an emotion?

That indicates your "primary modality". If you saw an image first, then you are primarily a visual person. If you heard sounds first, you are primarily an auditory person. If it was a feeling, you're a kinesthetic.

Here is where we get into the details—the submodalities. Again, while this may sound complicated, once you get the hang of it, it becomes very easy to work with.

Recall the same memory you used earlier. If you noticed an image first, was the image close, or far away? Was it in vibrant color, or shades of gray? Was it in the center of your mind's eye, or was it off to the side?

If you noticed a sound first, was it loud or quiet? Was it clear or muffled? Was it close or far away? If you noticed a feeling, was it heavy or light? Smooth or textured? Firm or soft?

These details of your primary modality are called "submodalities", and taking conscious control of them can be the difference between a prayer that does nothing and a prayer that produces miracles.

Okay, let's take this a step further. Think of something you would LIKE to experience, but you don't think will actually happen. Compare this to your earlier memory.

In general, most visual people find that questionable concepts come to them faded, seen from far away, fuzzy, and very much off to the side. Auditory and kinesthetic folks find similar differences when they think of things in which they have little faith.

Once you know how your mind uses the various sub-modalities to distinguish true from false—things in which you have faith from things you do not—you can use this information to make your prayers more powerful.

Basically, all you need to do is to imagine what you're praying for as if it were already true, using the same characteristics you found were common to factual memories.

In other words, if you're like most visual people, this means to imagine your preferred outcome in color, close to you, big and bright, with sharp focus, and in the center of your field of view.

Doing so will automatically increase your faith, and improve the results you get from prayer.

Instant Focus

Although I would prefer to avoid this topic, I feel it's important enough to bring to your attention. We humans have a natural tendency to come to a sharp focus any time we experience pain.

This is why some folks will literally bang their head against a desk, or slap themselves in the face. It's also the reason for the common suggestion to pinch yourself if you think you may be dreaming, because the pain of being pinched will quickly snap you out of a dream into a more focused state of mind.

Personally, I prefer to do a quick set of pushups or other light exercise, because it tends to have a similar effect.

BrainWave Entrainment (BWE)

Our modern world has produced a technology that can help you focus, relax, feel good, and bring you more in harmony with God, and do it all at once.   It's called BrainWave Entrainment (abbreviated as BWE), and uses specially encoded sound waves to "entrain" your brain into the desired state.

Millions of people have used brainwave entrainment for meditation, healing, activating intelligence and creativity, improving sports performance, and more. It's a safe technology that has been around for decades.

With a small investment, you can use BWE to help increase the power of your prayers. All you have to do is play the right type of BWE session in the background while you pray.

To help you understand this amazing technology, let me answer the most common questions.

What Are Brainwaves?

Everything in your body works in cycles. Your heart beats a certain number of times every minute, and your brain operates at various "cycles per second" with different frequencies corresponding to different states of being.

For example, right now as you're reading this, you're most likely in a "beta" state, and if scientists were to connect you to an EEG machine, they'd find your brain operating at between 12 and 28 cycles per second.

When you're relaxing or meditating, your brain is said to be in "alpha," or operating in the 8 to 12 cycles per second range. Further down the scale is "theta," commonly known as the hypnotic state, which includes the range of 4 to 8 cycles per second. Sleep is the deepest level, where your brain operates at under 4 cycles per second. This level is called "delta."

There's also another range of brainwaves called "gamma." This range is above beta, and starts at 28 cycles per second and goes up from there. And some folks use the term "epsilon" when referring to the range of brainwaves below ½ cycle per second.

In general, the slower your brainwaves, the more your mind is focused on internal activities, and the higher your brainwaves, the more your mind is focused on the outer world.

What Is Entrainment?

Entrainment refers to the phenomenon of one thing becoming synchronized to something else. A common example is when a tuning fork is struck, and another tuning fork of the same type starts to vibrate across the room. Another example is when two pendulum clocks are hung on the same wall. No matter how "out of sync" they are with each other at first, they eventually start to swing in perfect synchronicity.

In BrainWave Entrainment, pulsating sound or light is used in specific patterns to induce altered states of consciousness, such as those experienced in meditation, sleep, or intense concentration. BWE does not FORCE your mind into anything, but simply makes it easier to gently drift into these naturally-occurring mind states.

What Type of BWE Sessions Should I Use?

For meditation and prayer, a standard alpha session would work well. Since this is the type of BWE session typically used for meditation, you will find many companies offering suitable recordings for purchase.

Beta and gamma sessions are designed to speed up your brain, thus making it easier to focus. As such, they are often sold for the purpose of increasing intelligence, relieving depression, or as a treatment for ADD (Attention Deficit Disorder).

Ideally, for prayer you really want a BWE session that does both. These sessions are usually described as giving you a feeling of "alert relaxation" or "relaxed focus." Unfortunately, such BWE sessions are harder to find.

Depending on your goals, you may find that special-purpose BWE sessions can serve your needs more directly, such as boosting creativity and intelligence, reducing anxiety, and speeding up the healing process.

In the final chapter of this book, I describe a set of recordings I've produced to support you in your prayers. These custom-made recordings contain the ideal sequence of BWE frequencies for each intended use.

Success Momentum

This may not be strictly "instant", however, it does not require a significant amount of time either.

Before praying, take a few minutes to think of all the successes you've had in your life. When you do this, you naturally start to feel more confident in your ability to be successful again now and in the future. And since confidence and faith are essentially the same thing, this leads to greater prayer power.

These memories don't have to be excessively dramatic, like saving the world. They can be simple things, like successfully getting dressed in the morning, pouring a cup of coffee, or dialing the right number to talk to a friend. Of course, the more you are proud of your achievements, the better.

This is actually something you can do long-term as well. Just plan out a series of goals—starting with little things and gradually setting bigger and bigger goals—and as you reach them, your faith in yourself grows stronger and stronger.

As they say, success breeds success.

It's also said that the reason God gives us challenges is so we can overcome them and grow in our faith.

When choosing your own challenges, remember to start with something you can easily accomplish, and then gradually increase the difficulty one step at a time until you find yourself moving mountains with ease.

Light Exercise & Fresh Air

When I want to quickly regain my focus, I've found that one of the best ways is to get down on the floor and do several pushups. Another is to take a short walk outside. Both of these get my blood pumping, and increase the amount of oxygen and other nutrients getting to my brain, making it easier to focus clearly.

Closely related to this topic is maintaining your health through diet and exercise. Although this won't "instantly" increase your faith or focus, it's amazing how much of an improvement you notice after just a few days of eating well and getting good exercise. And as you might expect, this naturally leads to a more positive frame of mind, giving you more faith for prayer.

Rest & Recreation

Also along the line of "not quite instant", taking a few minutes to rest before praying is close enough to count. And taking a break for an hour or so to have fun will usually improve the results you get from prayer.

The reason this works is because we humans naturally have more faith when we feel good, and we generally feel better when we're rested, both physically and emotionally. We also tend to feel more in harmony with God when we feel good, and so taking time to relax and have fun is especially important.

If you enjoy taking a long hot bath, you may find that your prayers are most powerful while soaking in the tub. Or if you enjoy sitting by a fireplace, then that may be your most effective prayer spot. For most of us, eating and having sex are two activities that really put us into a positive frame of mind.

Basically, anything that makes you feel good can be an excellent way to prepare for prayer.

However, it's important to understand that you must be able to enter prayer with a spiritual focus, and not be distracted by physical pleasures. This is why many spiritual leaders teach abstinence. If a specific activity leaves you feeling distracted or less spiritual, it may be better to avoid it before prayer.

Chapter 4: Short Meditations for Greater Prayer Power

Although faith is the most critical aspect of Harmonic Prayer, having a sharp, clear focus ensures that you get what you really want, and not some half-baked version of it.

One reason why the importance of focus wasn't mentioned in the Christian Bible is because the slower pace of life back then made it relatively easy to focus, unlike our modern world, where distractions come at us from every direction. When you spend your days fishing or herding sheep, your mind tends to become very clear, without a lot of noise to interfere with your prayers.

With the pace of modern life moving at the speed of light, most of us have dozens, if not hundreds, of thoughts running through our mind at any one time. In fact, we have gotten so used to it, we don't even notice the constant noise inside our heads.

The problem with this is that if you have a dozen thoughts running through your mind during prayer, the message you want to communicate to God becomes garbled and confused, leading to less-than-desirable results.

Which means that if you want to develop your prayer power beyond a basic level, you'll want to take time to filter out the mental chatter that has become commonplace for most of us.

One of the best ways to accomplish this is with meditation.

Meditation has a long history, and is an excellent tool for improving mental clarity and developing a close harmony with God.

Although you may be surprised at how many benefits you get from a single meditation session, you'll want to make meditation a regular part of your life because the benefits grow substantially over time.

There are many forms of meditation, and in this chapter, I'll introduce you to a few of them. We'll start with one of the most common forms of meditation—one designed to achieve a mental state known as "no mind". This form of meditation is actually the most challenging, and the more you practice it, the more positive results you get from it.

Next, we'll go to the other extreme and work with a form of "active meditation" in which you stretch your perceptions to keep track of everything around you at once, which has the unexpected result of clearing your mind. In addition, this form of meditation activates dormant areas of your brain, increasing intelligence, memory, and creativity.

From there, I'll introduce you to a few guided meditations, which involve focusing on very specific ideas, and are used to achieve specific objectives. Guided meditations increase your ability to focus as you attempt to keep in mind many specific details at once, just like active meditation. They also guide you to explore various aspects of yourself, and help you bring yourself into greater harmony with God, thus further increasing the power of your prayers.

Each form of meditation is designed for a different purpose, and you'll want to experiment with all of them. If one doesn't seem to work for you, just move on to another, and come back to it later. Usually, once you've made progress with one form of meditation, the others become easier.

Many folks have a difficult time remembering the entire sequence of a guided meditation, and find that having a recording allows them to fully focus on each step in turn. If you would like to have professional recordings of these meditations, see the final chapter in this book for a special offer.

BWE-Assisted Meditation

Luckily, the technology of BrainWave Entrainment (BWE), described in the previous chapter, can be a tremendous help in meditation. This is the foundation for many products which promise to help you "meditate deeper than a zen monk."

The principle behind BWE-assisted meditation is that the BWE pulses naturally and automatically guide your brain into a very deep alpha/theta rhythm, which is the same level of mind reached by experienced meditators.

To gain this technology-based meditation assistance, simply play an appropriate BWE session while you meditate. As discussed in the previous chapter, this may be either an alpha/theta session, or a beta/gamma session, depending on what the meditation is designed to accomplish.

As you might expect, the recordings described in the final chapter all include the appropriate BWE assistance.

Passive Meditation

Despite it being the most common form of meditation, many people tend to avoid passive meditation because they feel it is "too boring," or "a waste of time." However, those who persist and learn to do it well are rewarded with an inner peace which proves to be extremely valuable.

When you've truly mastered this form of meditation, and can eliminate all distracting thoughts from your mind, your prayers become extremely clear and laser-focused, and produce phenomenal—even miraculous—results. The ultimate goal of passive meditation is to eliminate all thoughts from your mind, a state typically called "no mind."

If you're just starting out, you probably won't be able to simply turn your mind off, and you'll need to work towards an easier goal. In this case, you'll focus your mind on something simple.

Many people think they can easily focus on several things at once, and feel that focusing on a single item would take no effort whatsoever. However, they are often surprised to find that keeping their mind focused on a single thing—especially a simple one—is much more challenging than they first realize.

You may choose any simple item to focus upon, such as your breathing, your heartbeat, or a mantra you chant over and over again. An excellent mantra for this would be something like, "God showers me with abundant blessings."

Or you may choose a physical object, such as a candle flame, cup, pen, or piece of jewelry. These are commonly used by meditators to come reasonably close to the "no mind" state.

Whatever you decide to focus upon, the objective is to focus all of your attention on that one thing, and think of nothing else. If any other thoughts come into your mind, simply ignore them, and bring your attention back to center.

In the beginning, you may find that you need to bring your attention back to center every few seconds. That's okay. The more you persist, the less often you'll be distracted, and eventually, you'll be able to focus all of your attention on one simple thing for an hour or more.

When you've reached this point—which may take days, weeks, or even months of dedicated daily practice—you'll be ready to graduate to focusing on nothingness itself.

Well before that point, you will find that you generally feel calmer, more grounded, more centered, and able to think clearer. This starts to happen right away, even from just ONE meditation session. However, most people don't notice the effects until they have meditated several times, after the benefits become more pronounced. Once you start to notice the effects, you may find yourself wanting to spend more and more time in meditation.

As a general rule, you need to spend a minimum of 15 to 20 minutes in meditation for it to produce any benefits. You can extend your meditation sessions as far as you want, however, there is little point in meditating more than a couple of hours. A good balance is between 30 and 60 minutes.

Those who have practiced passive meditation for years often find that they crave it more than anything else in life. I encourage you to give it a fair try. Just 20 minutes a day for a month should be enough for you to discover how enjoyable it can be.

Active Meditation

When I first started learning about meditation, I found that my mind wandered far too often, and I never really experienced any benefits. Of course, I also didn't set aside regular time to practice, and attempted meditation only once in a great while. However, when I decided to try doing the exact opposite, the whole situation changed drastically.

As soon as I tried an "active meditation," my mind became extremely clear. I could suddenly see solutions for long-standing problems, and difficult concepts became easier to understand.

And this was all from a single 20-minute meditation!

The concept here is that instead of focusing on nothing, you attempt to focus on EVERYTHING. Every object in the space around you. Every sound you hear. Every tactile sensation, including the seat beneath you, the clothes you're wearing, the temperature of the room, and so on.

As you struggle to focus on everything at the same time, you create chaos within your mind. Out of chaos comes order, and eventually your mind realizes that the best way to focus on everything at once is to focus on nothing in particular. BAM! Instant clarity.

The best way to describe this is to consider a visual context. Whenever you look at a specific object, your focus is concentrated on that one object, and all other objects fade into the background. However, if you relax your eyes, and cease focusing on any specific object, then you can see all objects equally well with your peripheral vision.

What's really interesting about this form of meditation is that by pushing the limits of what you can keep in mind at the same time, you stretch those limits and become capable of keeping more in mind at once. In essence, your mind grows stronger.

This also means that with practice, your peripheral vision will pick up more and more details, to the point where you can use it as your normal mode of seeing.

This is the foundation for many speed-reading courses, which direct you to scan over pages in a book, allowing your peripheral vision to pick up the words as you go. With practice, you can eventually get to a point where you can read a normal size book in a matter of minutes.

As you might expect, this takes a high degree of focus, and may be considered a form of active meditation.

It's important to realize that active meditation—while highly effective for eliminating mental resistance and creating clarity—must also be balanced with rest and recuperation. Think of it as the mental equivalent of running. If you ran all the time, your body would quickly break down and you'd end up in the hospital.

However, with practice, you can extend the time you spend in active meditation, just as a runner can develop the ability to run marathons. In other words, build up your endurance over time.

Guided Meditation

This third form of meditation serves as a middle ground between the extremes of passive and active meditation. In guided meditation, your task is to follow a predefined sequence of thoughts and images. More details than passive meditation, and much fewer than active meditation.

Your success with this form of meditation depends on how accurately you follow the prescribed sequence, how clearly you imagine the steps, and whether anything distracts you from the process. The more accurately you can imagine the steps involved in the guided meditation, the more you train your mind to focus only on the things you want during prayer.

Guided meditation can be used to strengthen not only your ability to focus, but also your faith and feeling of harmony with God as well. The guided meditations in this chapter work together to form a complete prayer power support system.

It is generally recommended to sit someplace where you can be free to meditate for the time required. The meditations in this chapter usually take about 15-20 minutes, although they can be extended for a much longer period of time if desired.

Guided Meditation Examples

Divine Faith

This first guided meditation is one designed to build your faith to an incredible level—a level you may even call Divine. It is based on several of the concepts covered in this book, and is guaranteed to give your prayers mountain-moving faith.

Here are the steps:

1. Think of something you KNOW to be a fact, such as the reality of one or more physical objects around you, or the fact that 2+2=4.

2. Now think of something you know to be false, such as the idea that you might be a squirrel, or that you are sitting on the surface of the sun.

3. Pay attention to how you feel inside as you think of each of these ideas in turn. Notice how the feeling of truth differs from the feeling of falsehood.

4. Repeat the process with new ideas, and explore in depth how the feeling of truth differs from the feeling of falsehood.

5. Once you have a clear idea of how these concepts feel within your being, focus your attention on the feeling of truth itself, separate from the ideas which brought it to your attention.

6. Start using a variety of faith anchors, such as keeping your back straight, breathing deeply, and anything else that feels appropriate.

7. Imagine what the feeling of truth would feel like if it were magnified 100 times over. 1,000 times. 1,000,000 times.

8. Continue building this feeling as much as you can. Stay focused on it for at least 15 minutes before ending the meditation and going on to other things.

This guided meditation is one of the simpler ones, designed to help you identify and build the feeling of faith within yourself. The more you can bring this feeling into every aspect of your life, the more blessings you will find showering down upon you.

Divine Love

One of the most powerful guided meditations you can experience is one designed to bring you into more perfect harmony with God through love.

In this guided meditation, the steps are as follows:

1. Remember a time when you felt love strongly. If you can't remember such a time, imagine one.
2. Allow yourself to experience this memory until you feel love in the current moment.
3. Focus your attention on the feeling of love itself. Identify the feeling. Notice various aspects of the feeling, separate from the memory. Is the feeling warm, tingly, or bright? Does it have a sound, a smell, a taste? Describe the feeling in as much detail as you can.
4. Imagine this feeling of love growing stronger. Imagine all aspects of the feeling growing stronger, bigger, brighter, warmer, etc.
5. Continue to expand the feeling of love until it fills the entire space around you. Keep going until it fills the entire Universe with infinite intensity.
6. Bring your attention back to your body and the space around you. Open your eyes if they were closed, and perceive everything around you with love. (ie—if you see a chair, love the chair.)

7. Maintain the feeling of love as long as you can—for the rest of your life if possible—loving everyone and everything you see, hear, touch, smell, and taste.

This guided meditation will bring you into a more perfect harmony with the Spirit of God. The key is to magnify the feeling of love beyond anything you have ever experienced before, and allow this feeling to bond you with the essence of God in every thing and every person. The more you do this, the more powerful your prayers become.

Divine Power (Tree of Life)

Before the books of the Bible were written down on scrolls, the ancient Jewish people described both God and God's creation (the Universe) as a system of 10 circles and 22 connecting pathways they called the Tree of Life. Many scholars say this is encoded within the first 5 books of the Bible, as God gave it directly to Moses during the same time he received the Ten Commandments. They also say that meditating on this Tree of Life can be one of the most powerful ways to bring yourself into harmony with God.

Although there are many guided meditations possible with the Tree of Life system, in this guided meditation, you will focus your attention on the general form of circles and interconnecting pathways, as illustrated to the right.

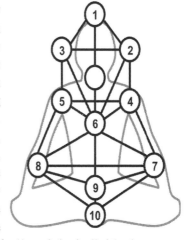

As you study the illustration, you'll notice an extra circle, between circles 1 and 6, around the throat area. This is a commonly used addition to the Tree of Life system, used to symbolize the connecting point between God (circle 1) and the individual.

You will also notice that the figure is sitting in what many call the "lotus position". There is no need to sit cross-legged during this guided meditation, or any other meditation in this book. Just realize that the 10th circle is located at your feet, and all the other circles stay where you see them, with circles 3, 5, and 8 to your left, and circles 2, 4, and 7 to your right.

Okay, here are the steps for this guided meditation:

1. Imagine a bright glowing circle of light just above your head. This is circle 1 on the Tree of Life illustration on the previous page. Imagine the infinite Power of God in this circle.

2. Imagine a shaft of Power extending down from the God circle to an area in your throat. See this Power filling another circle there. Feel it as vividly as you can.

3. See and feel this Power continuing to flow down the core of your being to your heart space—circle 6 on the Tree of Life. Imagine this circle growing bigger, brighter, warmer, more Powerful. Feel it. Make it real.

4. Sit for a moment, allowing the Power of these first 3 circles to empower your mind and body.

5. Now imagine God's Power flowing down from your heart space to the area of your genitals—circle 9 on the illustration—your sex center. This center is responsible for physical creativity, and channels God's Power into your creative activities, so you can be effective in co-creating with God on the Earth plane.

6. After a brief pause, continue to imagine God's Power flowing down to your feet—circle 10 on the Tree of Life illustration—where it becomes grounded in physical reality.

7. Sit and allow God's Power to vibrate the core of your being, from head to toe. This "middle pillar of balance" brings you into alignment with God, and gives you access to God's great Power.

8. Now, with this pillar of Power in place, imagine God's Power extending from above your head (circle 1) to a spot next to your left ear (circle 3). This is the beginning of the "pillar of severity" as it is known to those who study the Tree of Life. (God is both harsh and kind, and to be in true alignment with God, you must also be capable of both positive and negative forms of expression.)

9. Next, imagine God's Power flowing down to your left shoulder, to circle 5. Feel it. Make it real.

10. Continue by sending God's Power to your left hand, circle 8 on the Tree of Life illustration.

11. Now complete the circuit by sending this Power to your feet—circle 10. At this point, God's Power is vibrating your core and your entire left side.

12. With both the "middle pillar" and "pillar of severity" in place, it's time to build the "pillar of mercy" on your right side. Imagine God's Power flowing from circle 1 above your head to your right ear—circle 2.

13. Continue by bring God's Power down to circle 4 at your right shoulder. Feel the Power. See it.

14. Next, bring this Power down to your right hand—circle 7.

15. And again, complete the circuit by sending God's Power from your right hand (circle 7) to your feet (circle 10). God's Power is now flowing through you into the Earth through 3 different pathways.

16. Sit for a few moments and allow God's Power to realign your entire being and bring you into more perfect harmony with God.

17. As with our previous guided meditation, take this feeling of Power with you as you go about the rest of your day. Realize that you are more Powerful now than you ever have been in your past.

This is a great guided meditation because it has so many details involved. As you strive to keep all these details in mind at once, you gain an incredible ability to focus.

As mentioned before, the Tree of Life can be used for many different guided meditations. A popular one has you imagine the flow of Power through the circles in the order of their numbers, going from circle 1 to circle 2 to circle 3, and so on. This is said to represent the act of creation, and is called both the Lighting Bolt and the Flaming Sword.

Divine Wisdom

To create the ultimate (and truly "perfect") harmony with God, all three aspects of Love, Power, and Wisdom are required. Together, they form a musical chord resonating on multiple frequencies at once, establishing a fuller harmony with God than could be created any other way.

Love is the medium through which you connect to God and the Universe. Power is the force which performs miracles. And Wisdom guides you to get the best results possible in the shortest amount of time, while balancing many different factors that others may not even notice.

In this guided meditation, you will start with the harmonies created in the previous two meditations, and add the third and final aspect of God—Wisdom. Here's the process.

1. Start by eliciting a feeling of Divine Love, to harmonize with that aspect of God. The easiest way may be to simply remember what you felt at the end of the Divine Love meditation. Continue until you feel yourself resonating with the entire Universe.
2. Add to this the feeling of Divine Power. Imagine that the Power of God is flowing through your entire body, starting above your head, down through your core, and down both sides. Again, you may find it easiest to simply remember the last part of the Divine Power meditation.
3. Let the twin energies of Love and Power resonate within your being for a few moments, bringing you into a more perfect harmony with God.

4. As these energies resonate within you, imagine that they are activating dormant areas of your brain, creating new connections between the neurons, and raising your vibration. You may choose to imagine a light changing color and/or growing brighter within your head, or a sound increasing in pitch and/or volume, or maybe a warmth that grows hotter and hotter.

5. Continue focusing on this process of mental growth as long as you can. As you do this, your intelligence, memory, and creativity are all enhanced as you grow more in tune with God's Wisdom.

6. Next, imagine the entire Universe in front of you. Pretend that you can see everything from the beginning of creation to the end of time. It may be easier to imagine if you think of yourself as being outside of time and space, in a higher dimension of reality. In this way, you may see eternity as a very long strip of film, with the entire universe in each frame. As you take it all in, your mind grows even more to encompass the fullness of Divine Wisdom.

7. Bring the image of the Universe into yourself. Become one with it. As you do this, you create the connections required to access any information at any time.

8. Sit and allow yourself to become aligned with infinite knowledge, infinite experience, and infinite Wisdom. Know that you can call upon this wisdom at any time.

This meditation, more than the others, will bring you into perfect harmony with God, as you see and experience eternity from God's perspective.

Divine Mastermind

This guided meditation is designed to help you make conscious, practical use of Divine Wisdom. In this one, you imagine yourself as the CEO of a major organization (serving to manage your life, or your community) with God as your primary consultant, and a roomful of angels as supporting experts.

This is an excellent guided meditation to do when you need an answer to a problem, and want to get advice from the foremost expert on all things in the Universe.

Here are the steps:

1. Imagine you're in a conference room, with a large table capable of seating 20 or more.

2. On the table in front of you is a file containing everything you currently know about the problem facing you. The problem can be anything, from where you left your car keys, to putting an end to world hunger.

3. After you spend a few moments reviewing your file, the intercom beeps to let you know that your consulting team has arrived. The door opens, and in comes God, followed by a parade of angels. They take their seats around the conference table, which is now full.

4. Although God is your primary consultant, each angel has a specialty relating to the core problem. Every one of them places a file on the table, containing suggested solutions.

5. At this point, you open the discussion by thanking God for all the help you've received in the past, and expressing absolute trust that God has the perfect solution for the current problem. God acknowledges your gratitude, and expresses enthusiasm for the opportunity to help you again.

6. Now describe the problem, and explain how you will be happier and/or more capable of reaching your goals once this problem is solved. If others will also benefit, describe how they will be affected. It's perfectly okay if you're the only person who will benefit from having the problem solved. Remember, God wants you to be happy.

7. God now turns to each angel in the group to gather additional information and to formulate a solution. You

may or may not understand what they say to each other, but you know they are working out a perfect solution.

8. Once the entire group of angels has been consulted, God addresses you, and explains in very simple terms how you fit into the solution. If you need to do something, this will be explained. If the solution is complex, you may only get the next step in the process. Feel free to ask for clarification on any point you don't fully understand.

9. When you understand what you must do (if anything), thank God and the angels for their help, and call an end to the meeting.

10. Complete this guided meditation by imagining God and all angels leaving the conference room, going to take care of their part (or parts) of the solution.

Obviously, some problems are so simple, they don't require a conference room full of angels to solve them. However, having such a team of powerful allies working for you is extremely valuable. For example, the problem of finding lost keys—having a legion of angels means that they can look EVERYWHERE in a matter of moments and find your keys, no matter where they may be.

Divine Teamwork

This guided meditation is a slight variation of the previous one. In this one, you have a legion of angels ready, willing, and able to take care of any matter that will serve and support you.

There are no formal steps to this meditation. Simply spend time "daydreaming" about the possibilities of having thousands or even millions of angels at your beck and call.

Some useful things to imagine include assigning a group of angels to guard and protect your house, your car, and all your other possessions. You can assign whole groups of angels to protect each of your loved ones, guiding them away from danger, and serving to deflect any harm that may come their way.

Of course, you would also have dozens of angels as your own personal bodyguards, ready to jump in any time they are needed.

Feel free to assign teams of angels to perform specific tasks, such as maintaining your lawn, helping you find great deals, or whatever. They are there to serve you, as they know full well that serving others with love leads to happiness.

Give them something to do, and watch how quickly they jump into action.

Chapter 5: How to Grow Faith to the Nth Degree

A lthough the techniques described in the previous chapters will go a long way towards improving the results you get from prayer right away, there's a lot more you can do to maximize your prayer power over time.

In this and the next chapter, we'll cover a number of other things you can do to increase your faith. You can use these techniques to increase your faith in God, your faith in prayer, your faith in yourself, and your faith in things like "good luck." You can even use these techniques to increase your faith in having wonderful relationships, abundant wealth, and anything else you may want, which will make your prayers for these things much more effective.

The material in this chapter has been adapted from another book of mine, called *28 Days to Effortless Success*, which itself was based on an earlier work, *Choose To Believe: A Practical Guide to Living Your Dreams.*

Where Faith Comes From

When working to grow your faith, it's important to understand how faith develops. Where does it come from in the first place?

The first thing you need to know is that faith is another word for belief, trust, confidence, expectation, or knowledge. All of these words refers to the same basic concept applied in different situations. If you study what is usually taught about changing beliefs, you would get the impression that it's a difficult process, where you have to trick your mind into accepting an idea it doesn't want.

It's actually a lot easier than that.

You see, the process of acquiring beliefs is one we humans have perfected, and it's one of the main reasons we are the dominant species on this planet.

We acquire beliefs through a process of LEARNING.

Before I go much further, perhaps it would be a good idea for us to define what a belief is. This will help a lot.

A belief is an idea we associate with "truth".

If you believe that people are basically good, that means your mind has associated this idea with "truth" rather than "falsehood".

The same occurs when you learn new things, like when you first learned that the Earth is round and not flat, or that 2+2=4.

Learning this fact was not difficult at all. For most of us, the process went something like this:

- Here are 2 apples.

- Here are another 2 apples.

- How many apples do we have now?

- (after counting to verify) Yes, 4.

When we start dealing with beliefs about our own self-worth, or about our ability to get results when we pray, this process of learning may not be as easy to identify, which is why many folks feel (believe) that it's much more mysterious.

It isn't.

Somewhere along the line, we tried to do something. It may or may not have worked out the way we wanted. And we came away from that experience with a belief in our ability (or inability) to handle that type of situation.

And so, the next time we encountered a similar situation, we approached it with a belief about our ability to get positive results, and that tiny belief influenced our decisions, our actions, and consequently, our results.

If we had several experiences of failure, we may have even started approaching all new situations with a belief—an expectation—of failure. Many times, as I talk with folks about these ideas, someone invariably brings up a time when they approached a new situation with no clear pre-conceived belief about it, and yet it didn't work out the way they wanted.

In most cases, they mention this because they find it hard to accept the statement of "according to your faith is it done to you."

Here's how I respond:

When you approach a situation with no preconceived beliefs, you are open to anything—positive OR negative. When either experience is just as likely, then either one may occur. If you really want to experience miracles, you must consciously choose to believe in miracles, and approach every situation with an expectation of miracles.

Obviously, this is not the whole story behind the power of faith, and it would take a separate book to cover the whole story. If you're interested, I invite you to get a copy of my book, *Choose To Believe*, either from Amazon.com, or from my website, at: www.PowerKeysPub.com.

For now, know that changing beliefs can be easy. It's just a matter of learning something new.

Getting Faith from Others

When you want to experience something new in your life, one of the quickest and easiest ways to build your faith in it is to find evidence that other people have experienced the same thing in their lives. When you know that something has been done, and especially when it has been done by someone just like you, you naturally start to believe that you can do it too.

This is why marketers depend so much on testimonials and demonstrations. Whether it's a commercial for a diet program or a singles' website, or an infomercial for a new wonder-gadget, they know that the more you can see others just like you getting the kind of results you want, the more likely you are to buy what they're selling.

Of course, it's important that those offering testimonials are trustworthy. If you get the impression that they're just doing it for a paycheck, they lose all credibility.

In most cases, it's pretty easy to find evidence that others have experienced whatever you may want to experience.

For example, if you want to bring a new romantic relationship into your life, there are hundreds, thousands, or even millions of examples right in your own city where people have brought new romantic relationships into their lives. It's a common experience, so you don't have to go far to find such evidence.

However, if you take the time to ask people about how they did it, you'll hear a lot about chance encounters, luck, or even fate. You may hear about how they spent years looking for the right person before they finally found him or her, and you may even hear about a lucky few who ran into their ideal partner the very first time they tried.

The important thing to take away from all this is that IT'S POSSIBLE, and that the answer to your prayer for a new partner may manifest in a completely unexpected way.

As we discussed in Chapter 2, it's important to follow Divine Guidance after you pray so God can lead you to the perfect solution for you.

If your objective isn't so common, such as getting pregnant after 40, living to 120, or turning lead into gold, you may need to do a little more digging to find evidence that others have experienced the same thing.

One reason why many spiritual leaders suggest continual reading of the Bible is so you get accustomed to the idea of miracles occurring, thus strengthening your faith in them.

A Technique We Used in School

One of the most basic ways to learn new things, and therefore change the direction of your life, is to use a process generally called "affirmations".

Although the use of affirmations may seem to be a "new age" technique, it's actually something we used in school to learn new facts.

Do you remember these affirmations?

- In 1492, Columbus sailed the ocean blue.
- I before E, except after C.
- 30 days has September.
- The 3 angles of a triangle add up to 180 degrees.

Many of us learned multiplication tables by repeating them over and over again until the details were fixed within our memories. And then there's the ABC song with which we learned the alphabet.

Using affirmations in the context of increasing your prayer power is exactly the same. You repeat an idea to yourself often enough so it becomes fixed within your memory.

The only difference is that in this situation, your affirmations will look more like:

- God is all-powerful.
- God responds to my prayers with positive action.
- Day by day, I grow more in harmony with God.
- My mind is clear.
- My conscience is clear.
- I express my fullest potential in all things.
- My prayers get results.
- I have absolute faith.
- Miracles happen when I pray.
- I am valuable simply because I exist.
- I have a purpose in life.
- I fulfill a vital function in the world.

- God wants me to be happy.
- God showers me with abundant blessings.
- I am worthy of having everything I want.
- People accept me as I am.
- People like me and enjoy being around me.
- The past does not determine the future.
- I am incredibly lucky.
- Everything I do tends to work out for the best.

Although there are many suggestions about what makes a "good" affirmation, the best way I've found to craft your own is to imagine what you want to experience, and describe it as if it already exists, as you would if you were talking to a close friend.

The most important point is that your affirmation should be something you might say naturally in everyday conversation.

Don't worry if it includes any "negative" words. An affirmation which helped me get out of the worst situations of my life was, "It's not as bad as I think it is."

At that time of my life, I would not have responded to anything like, "God showers me with abundant blessings."

This is another major point with affirmations. In order to be effective, you must say them with a feeling of confidence that what you're saying is real and true.

If you feel that you're lying to yourself, it won't work.

At first, this may seem to be a "chicken and the egg" situation. How do you say an affirmation with confidence when it's something you don't yet believe?

Part of it is having confidence in the process. You know that the more you repeat an idea, the more you will believe it. And the more you believe it, the more you will see positive results in your life. In essence, you have confidence in the final outcome.

Another part is simply pretending. "Fake it 'til you make it." (A common affirmation, responsible for many successes.)

And of course, you can use faith anchors for this as well, just as you can when you're praying.

Adding Faith to Your Affirmations

Many people have experienced great success using nothing more than affirmations. However, some folks find the process difficult, because they don't know how to feel confident in something new.

We're going to fix that right here. And you may be surprised at how easy it is.

There are specific things anyone can do to elicit a feeling of confidence within themselves. For some folks, standing up straight helps them feel confident. For others, it may be wearing new clothes.

These types of things are what NLP students call "anchors", and these confidence anchors can help tremendously when using any technique designed to develop faith. You may recall we talked about faith anchors in Chapter 3.

Another way to elicit a feeling of confidence is to remember a time when you really WERE confident. As you bring the memory into your mind, the feelings come along with it. This is similar to the Divine Faith guided meditation in the previous chapter.

While all of these will work to build your confidence, they may not be easy to use when doing affirmations. What IS easy to use in this situation is another technique from NLP called "pacing and leading."

This process starts with you saying a series of statements you already believe to be 100% true. This is the "pacing" part of the process, and elicits a feeling of confidence and faith.

Immediately after saying the pacing statements, you "lead" the feeling of confidence to a new belief by saying your chosen affirmation.

Let's look at an example.

Start by listing a few things you already believe 100%. For me, the list may look like:

- 2+2=4.
- The sky is blue.
- I am a human being.
- I am now living on planet Earth.
- I am sitting at my desk.

You only need 4 or 5 pacing statements.

Now, write down the new belief you want to develop, such as:

- Miracles happen when I pray.

So, the whole list becomes:

- 2+2=4.
- The sky is blue.
- I am a human being.
- I am now living on planet Earth.
- I am sitting at my desk.
- Miracles happen when I pray.

The first few times you do this, you may want to take it slow. Say each statement aloud, and consider the truth of it.

- 2+2 really does equal 4, at least in normal math.
- The sky is blue a lot more than it's red, orange, or purple.
- Of course I'm a human being. I'm certainly not a squirrel!
- .... and so on.

When you get used to the process, you can speed it up to the point where you fly right through the list.

As with regular affirmations, these "pacing and leading" affirmations will need to be repeated over and over again until the new belief becomes fixed within your mind, associated with a feeling of trust and confidence.

The advantage of using the pacing and leading process is that you will always feel some degree of faith when you say your chosen affirmation, and building a new belief happens a LOT faster.

A New View on Faith

While affirmations may be the most common technique for changing what you believe in order to support powerful prayers, the technique we'll discuss here is much more powerful.

You see, one of the reasons why we have the beliefs we do, is because we have memories which PROVE them to be true.

If we believe we're terrible at spelling, it's because we have memories of being criticized for our spelling mistakes. If we believe we have difficulty relating to others, it's because we have memories of awkward moments with other people. If we believe we are more likely to fail than succeed, it's because we have more memories of failure than of success.

Luckily, this is relatively easy to change.

The solution is to create more memories of success, to the point where they outnumber the memories of failure.

One of the most direct ways to do this is with visualization, which may be described as a consciously directed daydream.

Now, before I start describing the visualization process, I want to emphasize that it doesn't matter if you actually SEE pictures within your mind. Visualization isn't just about images, and includes sounds, feelings, tastes, smells, and emotions.

Essentially, the way you normally remember things is how you want to visualize your new memories.

Of course, the more you can include as many senses as possible—sight, sound, touch, taste, smell, emotions, etc.—the better.

Right now, think of your mother.

- Do you see her face?
- Do you hear her voice?
- Do you feel her holding you?
- Do you smell her perfume, or the baking of bread or cookies?
- Do you taste her culinary delights?
- How do you feel, emotionally?

Notice how your mind has recorded the memories.
Now, imagine what it would be like to walk on a cloud.

- Do you see the cloud under your feet?
- Do you hear wind whistling past your face?
- Do you feel the wind on your skin?
- Do you smell anything?
- Do you taste anything?
- How do you feel, emotionally?

Next, turn your attention to something you'd like to experience in your life.

- What does it look like?
- What do you hear?
- What do you feel?
- What do you smell?
- What do you taste?
- What do you feel, emotionally?

Just by asking yourself these questions, your mind will be guided to create a new memory of the desired experience.

Again, the more you visualize positive, happy memories, the more you will believe that you can have more such experiences in the future, and the more your prayers will help you get there.

A More Refined Approach

Earlier, I shared a refinement to the old affirmation technique, making the process much more powerful and effective. Now, I'm going to share with you a similar refinement to the use of visualization, and it uses something we covered in an earlier chapter—submodality modification.

As we just discussed, when we do visualization, the goal is to create memories which are very much like the memories our minds create naturally. This makes them much more believable, and more likely to produce results through your prayers.

However, if you pay close attention, you'll notice that your mind stores memories differently depending on whether you believe them to be real or if you believe them to be merely fantasy.

It's almost like your mind uses blue ink to record things you believe, and red ink to record things you do not. In actual practice, it's more complex than that, but the concept is essentially the same.

As we discussed in Chapter 3, you can consciously control the way you focus on an idea to make it more believable simply by altering the submodalities, such as size, distance, position, clarity, brightness, volume, weight, temperature, and texture.

Here's an example. Let's say you are praying for a promotion or pay raise at work. To support your prayers, you may decide to create a series of new memories of your boss congratulating you for a job well done. This way, when you pray for the pay raise or promotion, you can easily feel confident that you deserve it, and will in fact get it.

If your primary modality is visual, you'll want to see your boss close to you, right in front of you (not off to the side), in vivid color, with lots of light, and make the images nice and big.

If your primary modality is auditory, you'll want to hear your boss congratulating you, with the words coming in loud and clear, from a position right in front of you, and with good tone.

If you're a kinesthetic, you'll want to feel your boss shaking your hand, maybe with a hand on your shoulder. You'll want to feel the floor beneath your feet, or the chair you would be sitting on. Feel the texture of any furniture or other object you would touch in that situation.

Whatever your primary modality, imagine the new memories as clearly as you would perceive them in the "real world". Use all your senses for greatest effect.

If you want to create new memories of being with a loved one, to support prayers for a new romantic relationship, you'll want to imagine being with your ideal lover, including as much detail as you can, with all the sights, sounds, feelings, and other senses coming in clear, sharp, and in full volume.

And yes, it's okay to fantasize this way, because it helps you pray for the things you want, and God wants you to be happy. If you recall, this is exactly how I prayed for the relationship I now have with my wife, Linda.

You can also use submodality modification to change weak beliefs into much stronger ones. When you notice that something has been recorded into your mind as a weak belief, you can imagine how it would be different with the submodalities changed, and you'll automatically believe it more.

You can go further and do the same thing in reverse, by taking negative memories and rewriting them in your mind as though they never really happened—as if they were nothing more than a bad dream.

And all of this gives you immense power over your belief system. Try it for yourself, and see how powerful it can be.

Growing Faith on Autopilot

Many years ago, people figured out that they could change what a person believed by presenting suggestions "subliminally". This means the suggestions are perceptible to your subconscious mind without being noticed by your conscious mind.

There is still a lot of controversy around this topic. Some people claim it doesn't work, while others make fantastic claims about what is possible.

Those of us who have extensive experience in this area tend to agree on one main point—in order for subliminal suggestions to work, they must be ALMOST perceptible to your conscious mind, but just barely out of range.

This explains why "silent" subliminals almost never work. (I say "almost" because there is always the placebo effect, which can produce results any time you expect results.) The same is true for backmasking (suggestions played backwards) and other artificial manipulations, such as suggestions that have been sped up to the point where they sound like birds chirping.

And while the subconscious mind is capable of processing an incredible amount of information, recordings which contain thousands of voices talking at once also lose effectiveness.

Visual subliminals, such as single frames within a film, have similar limitations. For instance, some video subliminals try to flash an image for only $1/1000^{th}$ of a second, which is far too short for even your subconscious mind to notice, and certainly too fast for any standard display device, such as movie film, TV, or a computer screen. The fastest display device (as of 2012) needs at least $1/120^{th}$ of a second to display a full image.

There are still debates about whether written words work when used subliminally, and this requires more testing. Personally, I feel they do, since this is the basis for many speed-reading courses.

In my own research, I've found that in addition to the above, subliminal suggestions should sound like natural speech, and be spoken by someone who clearly believes what they are saying. The more natural the suggestions, the more your inner mind will accept them as truth.

Creating your own subliminal recordings is fairly easy.

First, start by writing out a list of belief statements you want to program into your mind. For best results, these should be phrased in 2nd-person ('you' statements) because you'll hear them as if someone else is speaking. (And how often do you think someone is speaking about you when they use 'I' statements?)

Once you have a list, just record yourself speaking your belief statements, and then play the recording at a low volume so other sounds in your environment will "mask" the words. These other sounds may be nature sounds, your favorite music, or even a movie playing on the TV.

The more you listen to this type of recording, the more your inner mind will grow to accept the new ideas, and the more faith you will have that your prayers will be answered.

You may recall from Chapter 1 that one of my most significant financial breakthroughs came when I created just such a recording.

What we have covered in this book only scratches the surface of what you can do to strengthen your belief system. You will find much more in my earlier book, *Choose To Believe: A Practical Guide to Living Your Dreams*, available at: www.PowerKeysPub.com/choose-to-believe.

I have also developed an extensive system of audio recordings that may be used consciously or subliminally to build your faith in yourself and in positive things occurring in your life. This *EmBRACES Belief Entrainment System* may be found at www.PowerKeysPub.com/belief-entrainment.

Chapter 6: How to Eliminate Doubt

C hrist said that our prayers will produce miracles when we can ask for what we want "without doubt." If we have any doubt within us, it will interfere with our prayers.

The techniques covered in the previous chapter will work for most people, in the majority of cases. However, if you have a situation which is not responding to the Harmonic Prayer process, you may have serious doubts interfering with your faith.

In this chapter, I'm going to help you find the specific doubts which may be holding you back from performing miracles with prayer. In order to discover what hidden doubts you may have, you're going to need a tool. I call it a "belief scale."

Your Belief Scale

This belief scale will help you measure the strength of any belief. Once you understand how it works, you'll be able to identify whether a belief is going to help you or hinder you. Those beliefs which may hinder you are the sources of doubt.

Here's how it works.

Any time you ask yourself a question, your inner mind responds with an answer. We're going to use this natural response with some very specific questions to map out your belief system.

It's kind of like sonar, or radar, but within your mind.

The first step is to relax. The more relaxed you are, the easier it is to become consciously aware of the answers your inner mind provides.

The second thing you need to do is to realize that the answers you're looking for are not words, but a feeling. As you ask yourself these questions, you want to pay close attention to how you feel.

The first questions you ask are what I call "calibration questions." This is because they help mark out, or calibrate, the two ends of your belief scale.

These calibration questions can be anything, but they need to refer to things you believe are either 100% true or 100% false, and should not be anything else.

Here are a few examples of possible calibration questions:

- Do you believe you are a human being?
- Do you believe you are a squirrel?
- Do you believe that 2+2=4?
- Do you believe that 1+1=5?
- Do you believe the sky is blue?
- Do you believe the sky is brown with green polka-dots?

I think you get the idea.

The point here is to notice how you feel as you ask yourself each question. When you ask yourself about something you believe is absolutely true, you'll feel a different response than when you ask about something that's 100% false.

For me, I feel truth as an energy in my upper torso, and falsehood down in my gut. It's like an energy that rises or falls depending on how much I believe the thing being asked about.

Some folks feel a difference in temperature—hot or cold, a weight that is either heavy or light, a sound that's either high-pitched or low-pitched, or one of a hundred other possibilities. Some folks see a visual scale within their minds, indicating the strength of the belief in question.

You may need to spend some time asking yourself many different calibration questions to find your belief scale, especially if you've been in the habit of ignoring your feelings.

Take some time and practice this, because the rest of this chapter depends on you getting accurate information from your belief scale.

Using Your Belief Scale

Once you have a clear sense of where the two ends of your belief scale are, you can measure the strength of ANY belief.

The way you do this is to ask yourself a question (because your mind always responds to a question), and pay attention to your belief scale, because it will indicate how much you believe the answer which comes to mind. It's actually the exact same thing you did to calibrate the scale, except in this case, you don't already know the answer ahead of time.

For example, if you ask yourself, "Do I believe that I am worthy of having success?" your mind will give you an answer that could be yes, no, maybe, or something else.

Along with the answer will also be a feeling to indicate HOW MUCH you believe the answer.

So if your mind answers the above question with "I think so." and the feeling on your belief scale is close to the middle, you know your belief in that answer is weak, because your belief scale gave you a fairly neutral reading.

On the other hand, if your inner mind answered the above question with an answer like, "Of course I'm worthy!" and your belief scale responded very much like a positive calibration question, then your belief in your own worthiness is very strong.

If you want to be detailed about this, you can give numbers to the readings you get from your belief scale.

I tend to use numbers of 0 to 100, where 50 is the most neutral position on my belief scale. In my mind, I see this as, "My belief in this is 50/50. It could go either way," or if false, "My belief in that statement is absolutely ZERO. It can't be true," or if absolutely true, "I believe that statement 100%."

Some folks like to use -10 to +10, with 0 being a neutral reading. However you label your scale, just be consistent with it.

As far as using your belief scale to discover what you really believe, it's a good idea to calibrate your scale every 10 readings or so. This means that you would calibrate your belief scale, ask yourself 10 questions to reveal inner beliefs, then calibrate again for the next set of 10 questions. This helps to keep your belief scale accurate.

Below, you will find a variety of questions in three groups to help you measure the strength of beliefs in what I call the Surface-Level category.

It tends to be easier to identify Surface-Level beliefs, and this will give you good practice before we start digging deeper to get to World-Level and Universal-Level beliefs.

The most important part of this process is to be honest with yourself. Many people WANT to believe some things so much, they will lie to themselves and say they have a strong belief when they really don't.

I'll also share with you that EVERY single person who has attended my live workshops has been surprised by some of the beliefs they found using this process.

Here are the questions. As you measure the strength of each belief, give each response a number and write it down. If you don't want to write in this book, grab a sheet of paper, write the heading (Money Beliefs, Relationships Beliefs, etc.) and a list of ten numbers, Beside each number, write another number which represents the strength of the belief revealed by the corresponding question.

Group 1: Money Beliefs

1. Do you believe that you earn enough money?
2. Do you believe that money is hard to acquire?
3. Do you believe that you have to work to earn money?
4. Do you believe that one good idea can make you rich?
5. Do you believe that only dishonest people get rich?
6. Do you believe that the world's leaders determine how much money you'll make?

7. Do you believe that wealth is a measure of a person's contribution to society?
8. Do you believe that having abundant prosperity is normal and not any big deal?
9. Do you believe that you are worth at least $1 million?
10. Do you believe that you will receive $1 million this year?

Group 2: Relationship Beliefs

1. Do you believe that people respond well to you?
2. Do you believe that you fit in with others?
3. Do you believe that it takes work to keep a relationship?
4. Do you believe that it's easy to find a compatible partner?
5. Do you believe that there are many who are looking for someone like you?
6. Do you believe that you are a lovable person?
7. Do you believe that you must hide certain aspects of yourself to be accepted?
8. Do you believe that a relationship can be a source of continuous celebration?
9. Finish the following statement: to have a great relationship, I have to _____.
10. Finish the following statement: people like me tend to have _____ relationships?

As you can tell, the last two questions are different. How you fill in the blanks will also reveal what you believe, and can be a great tool to identify hidden beliefs.

Group 3: Health Beliefs

1. Do you believe that getting sick is normal?
2. Do you believe that the body heals itself naturally?
3. Do you believe that your cells are constantly renewed?

4. Do you believe that the body breaks down with age?
5. Do you believe that your DNA controls your health?
6. Do you believe that your body is a reflection of your consciousness?
7. Do you believe that miracles of healing have taken place?
8. Do you believe that miracles of healing still happen?
9. Do you believe that you could live forever?
10. Finish this phrase: to be healthy, I have to _____.

These three groups of questions will give you plenty of practice with your belief scale. When you find negative or weak beliefs, you can use any of the processes we discussed earlier in this book to turn them around and make them stronger.

Group 4: Self-Image Beliefs

I realize all this may seem like a lot of work, however, what we're doing now will pay off for years to come with a tremendous increase in the things you can do with prayer. If this work is too much for you, the final chapter will show you an easier way.

At this point, I'm going to give you a few questions to help you discover what you believe about yourself as an individual. I call this category, "Self-Image Beliefs."

These beliefs are more powerful than the Surface-Level beliefs we dealt with previously, because your beliefs about yourself as an individual will influence every situation you encounter, including new situations for which you have no pre-conceived beliefs.

As you might expect, these questions are merely a guide to show you the TYPES of questions you should ask yourself to uncover what you really believe on an inner level. If you're TRULY serious about improving your life, you won't stop with these questions, and you'll create your own.

1. Do you believe that you are a good person?

2. Do you believe that people generally accept you?
3. Do you believe that you deserve to be happy?
4. Do you believe that you have a good life?
5. Do you believe that you are gifted in some way?
6. Do you believe that you have a purpose in life?
7. Do you believe that you make good choices?
8. Do you believe that you make mistakes?
9. Do you believe that you have more problems than others?
10. What is "normal" for your life?

Again, the last question is different from the others, because it asks you to describe a generality. There are many ways to answer this question, but the core essence is to get at the general course of events you expect to happen over time.

For example, do you expect to be frustrated with other people, who never seem to want to go along with your plans? Or do you expect people to go out of their way to help you whenever you need assistance? Would you describe your life as an experience in limitation, or would "a never-ending stream of glorious blessings" be more accurate?

Changing the beliefs that come up with this and similar questions is usually best accomplished with visualization— creating new memories to support a more positive expectation of future events.

You now have four groups of questions to use in mapping out your belief system. Again, when you find negative or weak beliefs, you can use any of the processes we discussed earlier in this book to turn them around and make them stronger.

Group 5: World-Level Beliefs

As you may expect, you'll now ask yourself questions to uncover even deeper beliefs within your belief system. By now, you should have plenty of practice doing this, and reaching these deeper beliefs should be easier.

The beliefs we discover in this group are what I call "World-Level beliefs." These are beliefs you have about people in general, about what you can expect to experience when dealing with other people, and how this affects your life.

Surprising to many folks, your beliefs about people in general actually have greater influence over your life than the beliefs you have about yourself as an individual.

This is because your inner mind understands that you are a human being, and what is true for people in general is also true about you, at least in part.

This means that if you believe that people are lazy, self-centered, and often make mistakes, then you'll find yourself displaying those traits as well, at least to a degree.

Also, if you believe that people are self-centered and lazy, you will tend to make decisions which avoid asking for help. That will lead to dramatically different results than if you believe that people are usually kind, generous, and go out of their way to help a fellow human being. And whether you realize it or not, the results you get from your prayers will be very different depending on the direction your beliefs take.

Along a different line, if you believe that cancer develops at random, then you've allowed for the possibility that you may have that experience, even if you never think of getting cancer yourself. (God will often use your "random" beliefs to create "random" events in your life.)

That's why the more general beliefs are more important than those on a surface level. They set the stage for everything that happens in your life.

I realize this may be difficult for some folks to accept. That's okay. You don't need to accept this in order to get results from this book. Consider it part of the advanced material.

For now, know that your beliefs about "people in general" will influence the results you get in your life, both on a practical level (beliefs => decisions => actions => results) as well as from your prayers.

Okay, enough chit-chat. Here are the World-Level questions to ask yourself and get a reading from your belief scale.

Remember to calibrate your belief scale before going through the questions, and write down a number to indicate the strength of each belief.

1. Do you believe that people like to help others?
2. Do you believe that people are interested only in themselves?
3. Do you believe that only the strong survive?
4. Do you believe that cooperation is the key to success?
5. Do you believe that cutting costs is the best way to business success?
6. Do you believe that being excellent is a better path to success?
7. Do you believe that people are generally reasonable?
8. Do you believe that people are arrogant idiots?
9. Do you believe that the world is on the brink of destruction?
10. Do you believe that the world is becoming more and more enlightened?

You now have five groups of questions to think about. Again, when you find negative or weak beliefs, you can use any of the processes we discussed earlier in this book to turn them around and make them stronger.

Group 6: Universal Beliefs

I have one more group of questions for you, to help you uncover the deepest, most powerful beliefs in your belief system —your Universal-Level beliefs.

As you now know, these will influence EVERYTHING in your life, even though they may seem far removed from your daily activities.

And as you also know, these will be just a small sampling of the TYPES of questions you should ask yourself to map out your belief system.

Here you go. Remember to calibrate your belief scale for each group of 10 questions to get an accurate number reading.

1. Do you believe that there is a God?
2. Do you believe that God is a judge?
3. Do you believe that God is a teacher?
4. Do you believe that God is a playmate?
5. Do you believe that God is a protector?
6. Do you believe that God answers prayers?
7. Do you believe that we are all part of God?
8. Do you believe that life is a series of lessons to be learned?
9. Do you believe that life is a playground where all we have to do is have fun?
10. Do you believe that life is a jungle where only the strong survive?
11. Do you believe that we are spiritual beings having a human experience?
12. Do you believe that the universe follows strict physical laws which cannot be changed or broken?
13. Do you believe that precognition is merely coincidence?
14. Do you believe that miracles are real?
15. Do you believe that miracles are delusions?
16. Do you believe that magick is evil?
17. Do you believe in Heaven and Hell?
18. Do you believe that it's wrong to want things?
19. Do you believe that time is an illusion?
20. Do you believe that there is more to the universe than we can comprehend?

You now have six groups of questions to use in mapping out your belief system. I've given you a total of 70 questions to help you discover what you really believe.

If you want to take this to the Nth degree, you could start asking yourself questions about everything. Ask yourself if you believe the news reports. Ask yourself if you agree with your boss about how your work should be done. Ask yourself what would improve the relationships you have with the people in your life.

Each answer to each question can lead to other questions, where even more beliefs may be revealed.

As you are now well aware, when you find negative or weak beliefs, you can use any of the processes we discussed earlier in this book to turn them around and make them stronger.

Pinpointing SPECIFIC Beliefs behind SPECIFIC Issues

The process I'm about to share with you now is one that can reveal SPECIFIC beliefs behind SPECIFIC issues. In short, if you have a problem which is not responding to prayer, this process will show you EXACTLY which beliefs need to be changed in order to eliminate the doubt interfering with your prayers.

Some folks have suggested that I should charge a MINIMUM of $500 for this one technique, because it's so powerful. And yet, I'm about to give it to you at no extra cost.

There's a good reason for this.

You may have heard of a principle called tithing, which essentially means giving great value with the understanding that great value will come back to you multiplied.

It defies common logic, and yet all of the most prosperous people in the world practice it in one form or another. The best explanation of why this works is one I heard from Wayne Dyer. It goes like this.

Consider the Universe to be a mirror. If you are stingy and hold back, the Universe will also be stingy and hold your good back from you. However, if you are generous and give freely, the Universe will mirror your actions, and give freely to you.

It's not enough to just be *willing* to give. You have to actually do it. Think of it as God rewarding you for helping with God's work on Earth.

And that's why I'm giving you a technique which has proven itself highly valuable to many others. I call this technique, "Belief Archeology."

This process is relatively easy to do, but somewhat difficult to explain. The best explanation came out in the 2011 *Choose To Believe* workshop recordings. Here's the gist of it.

You start by writing out a goal. Something you would like to have in your life. It could be a specific amount of money, a romantic relationship, better health, peace of mind, or anything else you desire.

Once you have it written, you now ask yourself these two questions.

1) What's stopping me from having this RIGHT NOW?
2) What can I do to make this happen?

The first question will reveal the beliefs that are acting as obstacles, and the second question shows beliefs you can use to manifest your desired reality.

For each question, write down EVERYTHING you can think of that applies. This includes things which may otherwise be overlooked, such as the laws of nature and physical reality.

For example, if your goal is to experience vibrant health, a possible answer to the "what's stopping me" question could be "healing takes time."

This answer reveals that you believe in a physical process of healing, which would block you from experiencing an instantaneous healing miracle.

In some respects, you have to consider infinite possibilities, such as time travel, changing lead to gold, or walking through walls. When you approach this process with an "anything is possible" attitude, it's a lot easier to spot the limiting beliefs.

If you believe that these things are impossible (or just difficult to do), you will find your prayers less effective than if you truly believe that God can make ANYTHING happen.

And I think you'll agree that anyone who can create an entire Universe out of nothing can probably do anything you could possibly imagine here on Earth.

> *"I tell you the truth, if you have faith as small as a mustard seed, you can say to this mountain, 'Move from here to there' and it will move. Nothing will be impossible for you."*
> — *Matthew 17:20,21*

> *"Everything is possible for him who believes."*
> — *Mark 9:23*

When you ask yourself, "What can I do to make this happen?", your mind will answer with ideas you believe have a possibility of working. (ie—things in which you have faith)

If you act on these beliefs, you'll experience greater success than if you try to ignore them.

As an example, many people believe that one way to lose weight is to exercise more and eat less. If you follow these beliefs, you'll have an easier time losing weight than if you try to ignore them and wait for a miracle.

At this point in the process, you've written down your goal, and you've written down the answers your mind gave you to the two questions above.

That's the first level of this process.

The next level is to take each answer, turn it into a new goal, and repeat the process to uncover the deeper, more powerful beliefs in your belief system. Do this for each of the new sub-goals, as if they are a completely new process.

Keep digging deeper until you are unable to come up with a "reason why" a specific sub-goal cannot be accomplished. When you hit bottom, you've found what's known as a core belief.

When you've gone as far as you can with this process, make a list of the core beliefs you found. Then make another list of the next-higher beliefs. And a 3rd list of all other beliefs you found using this process.

From here, it's easy. Just use the processes we covered in Chapter 5 to turn these beliefs around to become strong, positive, supporting beliefs. Start with the core beliefs first, then move to the second list, and finally, if you still need to, work on the third list.

I say, "if you still need to" because many folks see results when working with the first two lists, and by the time they finish the second list, the problem is solved. Of course, I'm assuming that you'll be praying for a solution as well.

I fully admit that the instructions I've given you here may not be perfectly clear. You really just have to work with the process for a while before it makes sense. This is where going to a live workshop (or hiring a personal coach) comes in handy.

Chapter 7: How to Live in Perfect Harmony with God

S everal of the guided meditations in Chapter 4 gave you a taste of what it is like to be in perfect harmony with God. In this chapter, we'll discuss some of the ways you can extend that Divine Harmony into your daily life, and remove all limitations to your prayer power.

The suggestions in this chapter may at first seem to be based on a moral code of ethics. However, it is not my intention to impose any moral code upon you. These suggestions are here simply because they are the most practical ways to help you develop unlimited prayer power.

Unconditional Love for All

The teachings of Christ focused on two primary things—love and faith. Have faith that your prayers will be answered, and live with love for all people. Despite what many people may think, both of these teachings are highly practical.

As we've discussed several times in this book, the keys to effective, miracle-working prayer are faith, focus, and a feeling of harmony with God.

And one of the best ways to bring yourself into harmony with God is to live with love in your heart. This is why Christ said the teaching of the entire Old Testament ("the law and the prophets," as it was called in those days) could be summed up as what we now call "The Golden Rule."

> *"Do to others as you would have them do to you."*
> *— Luke 6:31*

Some people would say that Christ went too far with this idea, suggesting that we let people walk all over us.

> *"But I tell you, do not resist an evil person.*
> *If someone strikes you on the right cheek,*
> *turn to him the other also."*
> — *Matthew 5:39*

I will admit that the reason for this is not as clear as it should be. Paul makes this clearer in the following quote.

> *"Do not take revenge, my friends, but leave room*
> *for God's wrath, for it is written: 'It is mine to*
> *avenge; I will repay,' says the Lord."*
> — *Romans 12:19*

The idea here is that if you were to engage in violent or destructive behavior, then you would face consequences for your actions, even if you were just reacting to the actions of another person. It does no one any good to be like the child who says, "But he started it!"

In this, the Bible is hinting at the concept of karma, which says, in essence, that "what goes around, comes around." Live with love, and love comes back to you. Life with hate, anger, and judgement, and you get those back instead.

It's your choice. Take your pick.

If you want God to send you loving, generous people, then be a loving, generous person yourself. If you want people to go out of their way to help you, then go out of your way to help others. If you want people to forgive you when you make mistakes, then forgive others when they are in error. If you want people to respect you, then be respectful of others. If you want people to make you happy, then do what you can to make others happy.

As hard as it may be to believe, it works.

Guilt-free Living

Very closely related to the idea of living with love, the more you have a clear conscience and are happy with the choices you've made, the more you will be in harmony with God.

While there are many who will give you a great many suggestions as to what type of choices you SHOULD make in your life, the underlying theme behind most of them is "live with love and respect, and don't do anything to hurt another person."

To a large degree, this is nothing more than the Golden Rule expressed in another form. However, I want to address this topic separately, because many people have been taught a great many rules they must follow if they are to "avoid sin."

Now, I'm not here to tell you how to live. And I'm certainly not claiming to be the ultimate authority on "righteous living." What I'm talking about here is nothing more than living by a set of rules YOU feel are right, as they fit into the overall suggestion to live in harmony with God.

Inevitably in this type of discussion, a topic comes up which I tend to call "the lesser of two evils." One example of this is, "if you could go back in time and kill Hitler before he came to power, would you do it?"

Some people say it would be wrong to kill anyone, even if it means saving the lives of millions of others. Others look at the "big picture" and say that killing one rogue person can be considered good if it prevents a greater evil.

Personally, I take the second approach, as do all medical professionals when they kill bacteria and viruses to save a patient. If all life is sacred and to be cherished, as some people claim, then this would mean the lives of germs, bacteria, and other threats to human life would be just as valuable as any other form of life. And if one is comfortable killing millions of germs and bacteria to save one human life, is it so different to kill one human being to save the lives of many others?

In the case of a serial killer or habitual rapist, the decision is less clear. Could they be rehabilitated? Are we certain that they would continue hurting other people? Is it better to end their life, or force them to suffer a lifetime of incarceration? Where do we draw the line between serving humanity and enacting vengeance?

Luckily, few of us have to deal with such issues in our day to day lives. Usually, the decisions we face lean more in the direction of agreements and courtesy. How hard should we negotiate for the things we want? How much should we serve other people, and how much should we look out for our own interests? Should we walk out on a bad theater performance, thus showing less-than-perfect respect for the performers?

Again, I'm not going to make any specific suggestions, and will leave these decisions up to you. What I will suggest is that you take time to consider such things, and decide where you will draw the line between respecting others, and respecting yourself.

And once you determine the rules you feel are right for you, then live in accordance with them, without making excuses when it's not convenient or enjoyable to follow them.

Following through with your commitments despite hardship is a very important topic, and one we'll discuss in more detail in the following section.

Austerities

Many people who study spiritual matters run across the topic of austerities, such as fasting, celibacy, taking vows of silence or poverty, and other voluntary hardships.

There are two primary benefits to engaging in austerities. First, it strengthens your ability to focus, as it takes tremendous willpower to follow through with them beyond a basic level. Fasting for a month takes far more discipline than fasting for a day. And second, austerities help you turn your attention away from physical matters and focus more on spiritual matters.

The more you can focus on spiritual matters rather than physical ones, the stronger your harmonic resonance with God. And the more you can focus your mind, the better your prayers will work. Both of these lead to greater prayer power.

Austerities do not need to be life-threatening or incredibly difficult. Any rule you follow that is in the least bit inconvenient can also be used for the same purpose, although the benefits will be correspondingly less intense.

Anyone who chooses not to eat meat on Fridays, for example, is engaging in an austerity. So are those who choose to follow rules on how to dress, maintain their hair (long or short), walk two steps behind their spouse, or any of a hundred other rules for living that form the traditions of a culture.

Unfortunately, in our modern society, the reason for these traditions are not fully understood, and many people believe they are supposed to "keep us pure" so we can "measure up" and be judged worthy of God's grace.

While this COULD be a fair interpretation, it is far more accurate to say that following these rules helps us develop self-control, and in doing so, brings us into closer harmony with God.

What is NOT true is the notion that failing to follow the traditions would inevitably bring one out of harmony with God, and therefore cause them to lose the ability to get answers to their prayers.

In other words, engaging in austerities can be an excellent way to bring yourself into greater harmony with God, but it's not the only way. As you've learned in this book, there are a wide variety of ways to harmonize with God, such as the guided meditations in Chapter 4.

Practice the Presence

The phrase, "practice the presence" refers to a way of living first described by a Catholic monk named Brother Lawrence, who lived in the 1600s. The essence of this "living meditation" is that every moment of every day is filled with an awareness that you are with God, and that everything you do is for God.

Those who practice the presence of God learn to see everything as sacred and spiritual, including the most mundane and physical, such as washing dishes, cleaning floors, or taking out the garbage. When you can do your work with God and for God, it can never be meaningless activity, no matter what your work involves.

Whether you are the CEO of a Fortune 500 corporation, or the dishwasher at a fast-food restaurant, you fulfill a vital function in the world. Without you, the world would not work the way it should, and we would all be poorer for the loss.

Paul wrote about this concept in 1st Corinthians, chapter 12, verses 12 – 30 when he talked about how we are all part of the body of Christ.

> *"Now you are the body of Christ,*
> *and each one of you is a part of it."*
> *— 1 Corinthians 12:27*

Christ also talked about this concept when He said,

> *"I tell you the truth, whatever you did for*
> *one of the least of these brothers of mine,*
> *you did for me."*
> *— Matthew 25:40*

Every person on Earth is important in the eyes of God, and when we live with this understanding, we grow more in harmony with God, and our prayers become more powerful.

Put another way, the more we help others, the more we ourselves are helped by God. It is simply the most practical way to live.

Chapter 8: How to Get Maximum Results from Prayer

E arlier in this book, I suggested that praying for a million dollars may not be a good idea, primarily because the mental state which desires to stockpile such large sums of money (greed) is based on fear and a lack of faith in something which may be called "everlasting supply."

The reason why this isn't a great idea is because even if you get the money, the fear-based mental state would cause you to quickly lose it, and you'd end up worse off than you started.

In this chapter, I want to talk about the types of prayers which are likely to produce the reults you desire, and help you avoid the typical traps like the one mentioned above. Along the way, I'll also share with you some of the insights I've gained from my experiences with prayer.

What to Avoid in Prayer

Although it may be obvious to some, prayers which involve begging and pleading simply will not work, as they most certainly lack faith. If you truly believe that God will answer your prayer, then there's no reason to beg or plead for what you want. You just simply ask for it.

The same is true about the idea of making threats or demands. These types of prayers come from a place of anger and frustration, and while I can certainly understand how one may sometimes feel frustrated by Life, expressing such feelings in prayer is a waste of time. I know, because I wasted plenty of time doing it!

Because faith is such a central aspect to Harmonic Prayer, any mind state which lacks faith will cause your prayers to fail. Be calm and confident when you pray, and trust that God will provide a perfect solution. Imagine talking with a close friend who is always there for you.

Bargaining in Prayer

On the surface, attempting to bargain with God seems to also indicate a lack of faith. After all, if God is truly happy to help us with all we need and want, and God is the Source of All That Is, then there is nothing we CAN give back to God that God has not already given to us.

However, I want to clarify this, because the Bible suggests that there are certain circumstances where bargaining may be acceptable.

In Old Testament times, it was common practice to offer sacrifices to God in exchange for all blessings received. In fact, Christ himself told those who received a healing to go to the temple to offer the gifts required by Moses. *(See Mark 1:40 – 44 for one example.)* And when Christ sent his disciples out to their ministry, it was expected that those who received their blessings would provide them room and board. *(See Luke 10:1 – 12.)*

Obviously, God has no need of animal sacrifices, and gifts offered to the church are not forwarded to God. So why would the Bible stress such things?

The reason for this is because we humans need to remain respectful of God at all times, and if we were to start treating God as some sort of "errand boy," we would quickly lose our harmony with God, and our prayers would no longer have any power. It's also based on honoring the value of what you receive, either from God directly, or from those who serve as God's instruments.

Therefore, in order to maintain your ability to get results with prayer, you need to enter each and every prayer with a sense of respect and gratitude for the things God will do for you.

In Biblical times, this respect was mandated with a set of rules to follow—often involving animal sacrifices—much like the minor austerities we discussed in the previous chapter.

If your moral code of ethics says that you must give something of value every time you receive something of value, then you will get better results from your prayers when you offer to actively participate in God's work in exchange for an answered prayer. This participation is usually in the form of helping others, and may be expressed by donating money to a worthy cause.

Wisdom & Understanding

The Bible tells us that Solomon asked God for wisdom in order to serve his people, and in so doing, was granted many things, including wealth, health, love, and long life. So much did God give Solomon that he was considered to be the richest man in the world. *(1 Kings 3:5 – 14)*

This is a great reason to ask for wisdom and understanding before asking for anything else. In fact, I've found that my prayers for wisdom and understanding have produced the greatest value in my life. This is especially true when asking for the wisdom to help other people rather than just myself.

I believe the reason for this is based on the same idea we just discussed in the previous chapter—that we are all part of the one body of Christ. In other words, what helps one person, helps everyone. By helping others, you also help yourself, and the more people you can help, the more you yourself are also helped.

Another way of thinking about this is that when you actively participate in helping God bless the people of the world, God blesses you as well.

Asking for wisdom and understanding goes further than this, because when God gives you wisdom, you are able to find solutions to problems which confound even the most highly-trained experts. And when you become good at solving problems, your success is practically guaranteed. Sometimes, the simplest solution to a conflict becomes obvious when you understand the other person involved.

Strength & Skill

Having the wisdom to find a solution is only part of the process. The next step is to have the courage, strength and skill to implement that solution. For some of us, just asking for help or directions can take a significant amount of effort. ☺

In many cases, you are given problems so you can develop strength and skill in the process of solving them. You could say it is God's way of motivating you to live up to your potential. You could also consider it to be a "training program" in which you are being groomed for greater things.

The greater your destiny, the more intense your training.

If God did all the work to solve your problems for you, you wouldn't get much out of the experience. However, God is perfectly happy to help you, and will give you what you need when you ask.

Almost everyone has heard the story of a 98-pound woman lifting a car to save her son. Or the incredible feats of strength demonstrated by Samson in the Bible.

Luckily, very few of our problems require such literal strength. In most cases, the strength we need is psychological, and may be called courage, assertiveness, integrity, honesty, or diplomacy.

For example, you may find that the solution to your money problem requires that you ask your boss for a raise. If this is frightening for you—so much so that it holds you back—then you may find it worthwhile to pray for the strength to face your boss and ask for what you deserve.

If your problem is one of loneliness, and your love life consists of a long series of first dates, then you may need the strength to take an honest look at your own personality, and how you may be driving away potential partners. There may be plenty of other fish in the sea, but how much time do you want to spend fishing?

Once you've gained the strength to tackle a problem, you may also need to develop new skills to solve it successfully. In business arenas, this may require learning how to speak in front of an audience, or how to attract profitable customers. In romantic relationships, it may be developing the skills of listening and showing genuine interest in the other person's feelings.

Here again, God is ready, willing, and able to help you develop the skills you need. When you pray for help to solve your own problems, you're much more likely to get the results you want than if you simply sit back and ask God to do it for you.

When you and God work together, amazing things happen.

One of the great things about praying for strength and skill is that they, like wisdom, pay off huge dividends over time. The more wisdom, strength, and skills you possess, the more you are capable of getting anything you may desire in your life.

Something missed by many people is the option to pray for the strength and skills of increased faith, improved focus, and greater harmony with God—in essence, praying for greater prayer power.

Help & Protection

God understands that you will not always be able to solve your own problems, even with Divine Guidance. Sometimes the help you need involves things you cannot handle on your own, or protection from things outside of your awareness.

When you are sincerely doing everything you can to solve your problems, and pray for general help and protection, God can provide assistance in ways you cannot imagine.

Let's take a simple example here—as a part of your daily prayer session, you ask God to protect you from all harm. During your day, you may experience an unusually long delay as traffic is held up by a stray dog and her puppies, which happened to run out into the road just moments before you arrived. Unknown to you, the delay was necessary to prevent you from having an accident further up the road.

Asking for help and protection doesn't need to be limited to specific situations. Regularly asking that God watch over you and protect you from all harm is good advice, and can produce quite interesting results.

I've lost track of the number of times some strange occurrence happened in my life, after which I discovered that if it had not happened, I probably would have been hurt. It has gotten to the point where I almost don't even question when things don't go the way I had intended, because when that happens, it's usually because God is looking out for me.

Supply

The first request in the Lord's Prayer *(Christ's suggestion of how we should pray)* was for supply. "Give us today our daily bread." In fact, this phrase gives us an excellent example of HOW we should pray for the things we need.

Notice that Christ does not suggest we pray for *tomorrow's* bread, but for today's only. There are two ways to interpret this.

The first is that we should focus our attention on the moment, and not be concerned for the future, because the future will take care of itself.

> *"Therefore do not worry about tomorrow,*
> *for tomorrow will worry about itself.*
> *Each day has enough trouble of its own."*
> *— Matthew 6:34*

This is the primary reason why I recommend against praying for a million dollars so you can live the rest of your life in comfort and style. If you want a life of comfort and style, then pray for it specifically. Be direct. And then trust that God will guide you in whatever ways are necessary to make it happen.   Once you achieve the lifestyle you want, reinforce your prayer on a regular basis, just as the prayer for daily bread.

The other way to interpret Christ's suggestion to pray for today's needs and not tomorrow's is that God will answer our prayers quickly, and we can count on speedy results.   In fact, the Bible tells us that God answers prayers BEFORE we even ask.

> *"Before they call I will answer;*
> *while they are still speaking I will hear."*
> — *Isaiah 65:24*

When you realize that God is not limited by space or time, and that literally ANYTHING is possible, it becomes easy to understand how God can actually answer our prayers before we even make them.

The Reason Why

When praying for something, the reason why you're praying for it is much more important that what it is.   This is because the motivation behind a prayer can sometimes interfere with your harmony with God, and could therefore potentially block your prayer from producing any results.

If you recall from the previous chapter, one of the factors contributing to your harmony with God is living according to the rules you believe are right.   Living without guilt, or to put it another way, having a clear conscience.   If your prayer is motivated by a desire deemed wrong by your moral code, then your harmony with God will be weaker, and the prayer won't work as well as it could.

For example, if your moral code says that things like greed, pride, or lust are wrong (which is suggested in several places throughout the Bible), and if you were to pray for something that reflects one of these mind states (such as a fancy car to show off around the neighborhood), then your prayer would be blocked. Again, I'm not here to tell you what you SHOULD pray for, and am simply offering a few suggestions based on what I've experienced in my life.

Global Enlightenment & Healing

There are two primary reasons why you may want to consider praying for global enlightenment and healing.

The first goes back to a topic we've discussed several times throughout this book. The more you actively help other people, the more God helps you. By praying for the well-being of the entire human race, you are setting up a wonderful harmonic resonance that will reverberate through your entire life.

Those who believe in karma—the principle of "what goes around, comes around"—will quickly see how praying for global enlightenment and healing creates massive amounts of "positive karma" which will come back as many wonderful blessings.

The second reason why you may want to consider praying for global enlightenment and healing is because praying for such a large group of people tends to put you into the ideal mental state for prayer, especially when you're still learning what effective prayer feels like.

This is because effective prayer requires a level of "Divine Detachment"—a feeling of faith that the problem is already solved and nothing more is required—which may be more difficult to achieve when you are personally involved.

For both of these reasons, I start the majority of my prayers with a request for global enlightenment and healing. Not only does it help me get into the right frame of mind for effective prayer, it also creates positive karma to come back to me as an answered prayer for myself.

Open-ended Results

Whenever you pray for anything, it's a good idea to leave the specifics to God, and focus on the essence of what you want.

The core idea here is that God knows more than any of us, and if we try to dictate how God should answer our prayer, then we'll actually be blocking it from happening as easily as it could.

For instance, if you meet someone you really like—so much so that you feel you'd like to marry this person—I'm suggesting you don't ask God to make this one specific person fall in love with you. Rather, ask God to help you marry someone who embodies the things you like about this person, such as a cute smile, bubbly personality, or quirky sense of humor.

Again, as with most things, there are two main reasons for this. First, by leaving the details to God, you could very well be introduced to someone you enjoy MORE than the person you currently know. And second, attempting to FORCE a specific person to do something they may or may not want to do goes against one of the main principles of being in harmony with God, which is to love everyone as suggested by the Golden Rule.

In the case of asking for a specific type of person to marry, your prayer may cause the person you know to fall in love with you, or it may lead you to meet someone else who will. Either way, you get what you really wanted—marriage with someone who embodies specific traits and characteristics. By leaving the details to God, you get more of what you want, faster and easier.

Even if your request doesn't involve another person, it's a good idea to leave the specifics to God, because God may know how to bring you the essence of what you want in another way.

Let's say you get the idea to start your own business because you want the freedom to take vacations whenever you want. It's a better idea to pray for time freedom and frequent vacations rather than praying for business ownership. The reason for this is because many who start their own business actually have much LESS time available for recreation than they had as employees, as

they find themselves with many more responsibilities and
deadlines.

For the same reasons, it's better to pray for overall good
health than to pray for a specific condition to be healed. A
specific condition may simply be a symptom of a larger health
problem. By praying for overall good health, God is then free to
heal anything and everything in your body that isn't working at
peak efficiency.

If we take this idea to it's logical conclusion, we get ...

One Prayer for Everything

Most of us have a long list of things we want, including
money, love, respect, vibrant health, long life, excitement,
adventure, creative expression, and so on.

It's possible to reduce everything you want in life to a single
prayer request—to be happy. If you pray for happiness above all
else, and give God the freedom to manage the details, you may be
surprised at how much more enjoyable Life becomes.

> *"But seek first his kingdom and his*
> *righteousness, and all these things will be given*
> *to you as well." — Matthew 6:33*

Many folks, such as mystics, monks, and nuns, can be
perfectly happy with virtually nothing. When you know that you
fulfill a vital function in the world, and that God is ready, willing,
and able to provide you with anything you may need or want, it's
easy to relax and "just go with the flow."

This isn't to suggest that praying for other things is wrong.
Far from it. I'm just suggesting that when you don't know what to
pray for (or what to pray for first), that you consider praying for
happiness, and let God work out the details.

Chapter 9:
Prayer Support

S omething we've discussed often in this book is that when you take an active role in doing good things for others, God will do good things for you. In this final chapter, I want to talk about how you and I can support each other and the world at large through prayer.

We've already discussed how praying for global enlightenment and healing may be one of the best prayers to make. We've also talked about how the more you pray, the better you get at it.

In March 2012, I started a prayer support group. Those who register a prayer request get one or more prayers specifically intended to help their individual situation, and then they are included in prayers for the group as a whole for as long as they remain a member.

I am still offering this service. The prayer request form is located at www.PowerKeysPub.com/prayer-support.

The prayer support service is free to all who need it. My time is paid for through the sale of books like this one and other products I make available on the PowerKeys Publishing website, as well as through donations offered by kind and generous folks who wish to support my work.

And no, I'm not asking you to send in a donation, although if you wish to do so, I certainly won't stop you.

What I'm suggesting is that if you feel you need prayer support from me, feel free to register your request on the page mentioned above. I'm happy to support you with my prayers.

I'm also suggesting that you take time and offer prayers for others. These prayers may be for folks you know—family and friends—or they may be for folks you have never met. You may offer prayers for people affected by natural disasters, people who are in positions of governmental power, or for people who have lost their way.

As long as your prayers are motivated by a genuine interest to help others, they can only do good things.

If you wish to contact me—either to ask for clarification on anything in this book, or to tell me of a miracle that happened after you prayed for it—the best way is to use the contact form on my main website, at: www.PowerKeysPub.com/contact.

Be blessed, and know that I'm praying for you.

The Harmonic Prayer Support System

For those who wish to get faster results with Harmonic Prayer, I have created a set of audio recordings to make using the system easier.

Everything described here is a part of the *Essential Harmonic Prayer Support Package*. There is also a Deluxe Package available for those who wish to further maximize their results.

If you're interested in these audio programs, you'll find them at www.PowerKeysPub.com/harmonic-prayer.

Faith CDs (4)

To help you increase your faith, I have included in the Essential support package four CDs from my *EmBRACES Belief Entrainment System*. These CDs were designed to be played in the background while you do other things (such as working, driving, or other activities requiring focus), and reinforce the beliefs required for strong faith in magic and miracles—exactly what most folks want from their prayers.

What's really great about these CDs is that they contain so much variety, you will never get "desensitized" to the material. This means that you will continue to get positive results no matter how long you listen to them.

For a complete description of the technologies contained in these *EmBRACES* recordings, go to:
www.PowerKeysPub.com/belief-entrainment.

Feeling CD

To help you increase your feeling of being in harmonic resonance with God, I have created a set of four guided meditations. All of these meditations include a BWE (BrainWave Entrainment) component, which helps put you into the ideal mind state for meditation.

Harmonic Meditation for Divine Faith – This 20-minute meditation helps to increase your faith as well as the feeling of harmony with God. It guides you through a proven process to identify the feeling of faith, and then to amplify it to the point where you KNOW that you can perform miracles.

Harmonic Meditation for Divine Love – One of the most powerful factors for achieving harmonic resonance with God, this 20-minute meditation guides you through a process which connects you with the most powerful love in the Universe.

Harmonic Meditation for Divine Power – This 20-minute meditation uses a Kabbalah form called the "Tree of Life", said to be the most powerful way to bring yourself into harmonic resonance with God. This meditation does not stop with the middle pillar of balance as most do, and also includes the pillar of severity and pillar of mercy as well. By the time you're done with this meditation, you'll FEEL God's Power vibrating throughout your entire body!

Harmonic Meditation for Divine Wisdom – The final 20-minute meditation on this CD, this meditation completes the process of bringing you into PERFECT harmonic resonance with God, as it combines Divine Love and Divine Power to activate dormant areas of your brain and mind, creating new connections between the neurons, and increasing your intelligence, your memory, and your creativity, as you grow more in tune with the Divine Mind of God.

Feel free to listen to these meditations individually, or all at once. Either way releases incredible prayer power!

Focus CD

To help you increase your ability to focus, and thereby clearly communicate what you want in prayer, I have created a series of three meditations.

Passive Meditation – This 20-minute meditation guides you into a traditional passive meditation, where you eliminate all distracting thoughts from your mind. This process is helped by a BWE (BrainWave Entrainment) track, which automatically takes you into a low alpha state of mind.

Active Meditation – This 20-minute meditation goes in the opposite direction, and guides you through a process where you eventually pay attention to EVERYTHING in the environment around you. Your limits will be pushed and stretched, as you grow to become more than you were. This meditation has produced extraordinary results for those who have used it.

BWE Brain Tune-up – This 30-minute BWE session contains no words, yet removes any resistance within your brain, allowing you to think faster, more clearly, and using less energy. As a result, you find yourself sleeping less, getting more done, and achieving better results. Incredible!

Prayer Session CD

This CD—intended to help you focus your mind during prayer—automatically makes your prayers more powerful. These sessions may also be used for self-guided meditations. They help focus your mind using BWE (BrainWave Entrainment), a natural technology proven to help you reach deeper levels than you could on your own. There are four 20-minute tracks on this CD.

Alpha Track – This track uses a basic alpha BWE protocol with music, giving you a gentle background with which to pray. Perfect for those new to BWE.

Alpha+Theta Track – This track goes deeper, and helps you focus even more, to the point of disconnecting from the world around you. The background contains natural forest sounds.

Alpha+Theta+Gamma Track – Similar to the above track, this one adds a gamma component, to prevent you from "zoning out" to the point of losing your intention. Especially useful for those who tend to fall asleep during meditation. The background here is a natural beach environment.

Theta+Gamma Track – For those who want to explore the limits of BWE-enhanced prayer and meditation. This session takes you deeper, while keeping you focused. Includes other-worldly music to help you further disconnect from current reality.

BWE Session CD

In addition to all of the above, the *Essential Harmonic Prayer Package* includes this resource CD, with four different BWE sessions to help you get positive results in all areas of life. None of these session include any words, and the effects are purely from the technology of BrainWave Entrainment. Also, headphones are NOT required for any of these sessions, making them easier to use any time you want.

Creativity Booster – This 20-minute BWE session will break you out of any box of limited thinking you may be stuck in. Using a series of random BWE frequencies, your brain will be slowed down, sped up, and taken for a ride so you can see your problem from many points of view all at the same time. Creative solutions tend to pop out just like toast from a toaster!

IQ Booster – This 20-minute BWE session activates dormant area of your brain using a highly specialized BWE protocol in the upper-beta range. Scientific studies have shown that many people gain an average of 30 IQ points from listening to this protocol once a day for a week.

Healing BWE Session – This 20-minute BWE session uses two distinct BWE tracks to activate the natural healing process in your body. For best results, listen to this session three times or more in succession for maximum effect.

Anxiety Relief – This 20-minute BWE session is especially useful for those who find it difficult to relax. Starting at a high-beta, this session slowly brings you down into a more relaxed alpha state before bringing you back to a low-beta at the end. As a result, you'll be calm, confident, and alert.

Again, all of these recordings are part of a special support system I've created for you to get maximum results from the Harmonic Prayer process as quickly as possible. This system may be found at: www.PowerKeysPub.com/harmonic-prayer

Thank you.

Also Available From PowerKeys Publishing

Choose To Believe

The core foundation of Alan Tutt's work, *Choose To Believe* provides a scientific and practical understanding of the power of faith. In this book, you'll learn:

- What science has to say about the Power of Faith
- How beliefs become "real world" experience
- How to find and measure your true beliefs
- How to change what you believe and enjoy life more
- How to covertly help others change what they believe

Essential Package

- *Choose To Believe* ebook
- *28 Days to Effortless Success* ebook
- 2008 Choose To Believe workshop audio recordings
- 2011 Choose To Believe workshop audio recordings

Deluxe Package

Includes the complete Essential Package above, plus:

- Complete Self-Esteem module from *EmBRACES Belief Entrainment System* (36 recordings)
- *Law of Attraction Insider* teleseminar series (23 recordings plus transcripts)
- 5 additional teleseminars featuring Alan Tutt.

All of the above are fully described at www.PowerKeysPub.com/choose-to-believe.

EmBRACES Belief Entrainment System*

For those who want maximum results with minimum effort. The *EmBRACES Belief Entrainment System* includes 360 recordings of background audio (120 full CDs worth) which combine BWE, NLP, NSS, and 492 belief statements to condition your mind for true success. Covers all areas, from self-esteem and self-sufficiency, to confidence, motivation, productivity, self-mastery, peace of mind, relationships, and prosperity.

One of the main problems with most mind-conditioning materials is that they repeat a handful of statements over and over again with the same voice and the same music. As such, your inner mind quickly identifies it as a repeating pattern, and tunes it out before it has a chance to produce any results.

With the *EmBRACES Belief Entrainment System*, multiple voices are used, with a wide variety of music and tones to create a highly textured audio experience which remains non-distracting, yet keeps your inner mind engaged and listening. This maximizes the results you get.

Further enhancing your self-development, the belief statements are not subliminal, but are presented in a low-key manner which presents minimal distraction. This "not-so-subliminal" (NSS) approach has been proven to work time and time again.

Each recording in the EmBRACES Essential Package includes a BrainWave Entrainment (BWE) track which gently shifts your brain into a highly relaxed and receptive state, the ideal state for learning new material.

Both of the above packages are fully described at www.PowerKeysPub.com/belief-entrainment.

* – EmBRACES stands for:
Empowering Belief Reinforcement and Alignment for
Confidence, Excellence, and Success.

Awaken the Avatar Within

Similar to *Harmonic Prayer*, *Awaken the Avatar Within* (due to come out in 2012) presents its material without the religious overtones.

For more information on this book and associated packages, go to www.PowerKeysPub.com/awaken-the-avatar-within.

Prosperity From the Inside Out

Taking the core ideas from *Choose To Believe* and addressing the issue of prosperity directly, *Prosperity From the Inside Out* starts by addressing the specific beliefs required for abundant prosperity, and then expands by covering a variety of practical tips and tricks for attracting money from every direction.

Treasure Map to Online Riches

The Internet has been responsible for more "overnight millionaires" than anything else in history. In this 157-page report, Alan Tutt explains the key principles involved in building an online business that is practically guaranteed to be a success.

Covering everything from basic concepts, to step-by-step instructions for setting up a profitable website, to high-end marketing principles previously available only in $2,000 courses, *Treasure Map to Online Riches* is literally a gold mine of high-value information.

Both of the above books, plus associated packages, may be found at www.PowerKeysPub.com/prosperity.

PowerKeys Pointers Mailing List

To stay up to date with everything that happens on the PowerKeys Publishing website, including new releases, sign up to our mailing list at www.PowerKeysPub.com/powerkeys-pointers.

Quantity Discounts

Do you have a study group and would like to save money on books? Or are you planning a fund-raiser and want to feature something new and exciting? Or does your business need a large quantity of low-priced items to use as sales incentives?

If any of these describe you, PowerKeys Publishing can help with our generous quantity discount program.

For small groups, buy 4 or more books, and get the standard bookstore discount of 40%. If you buy 20 or more, you get the full wholesale discount of 50%.

Those needing larger quantities can move up to our corporate or distributor levels with discounts of 60% and 70% respectively. To qualify, your purchase must be 100 or 500 copies of the same book.

Here's a chart to make it easy to figure your discount:

Minimum # of Copies	Discount off regular price
4	40%
20	50%
100	60%
500	70%

Quantity discounts are automatically applied when placing orders on the PowerKeys Publishing website. If you need (or want) any assistance, just use the contact form on the website. www.PowerKeysPub.com/contact